EARTHQUAKE ARCHITECTURE

New construction techniques for earthquake disaster prevention

EARTHQUAKE ARCHITECTURE

New construction techniques for earthquake disaster prevention

Publisher
Paco Asensio

Editor
Belén García

Translators
William Bain
Harry Paul

Copy editor
Wendy Griswold

Proofreader
William Bain

Art director
Mireia Casanovas Soley

Designer
Emma Termes Parera

Layout
Jaume Martínez Coscojuela

Hardcover ISBN:
0-06-019890-7

First published in 2000 by LOFT and HBI,
an imprint of HarperCollins Publishers.
10 East 53rd St.
New York, NY 10022-5299

Distributed in the U.S. and Canada
by Watson-Guptill Publications
770 Broadway
New York, NY 10003-9595
Telephone: (800) 451-1741 or (732) 363-4511 in NJ, AK, HI
Fax: (732) 363-0338

Distributed throughout the rest of the world
by HarperCollins International
10 East 53rd St.
New York, NY 10022-5299
Fax: (212) 207-7654

Printed in Spain:
Gráficas Apipe

Editorial project
Loft Publications s.l.
Domènech 7-9, 2° 2ª
08012 Barcelona, España
Tel.: +34 93 218 30 99
Fax: + 34 93 237 00 60
e-mail: loft@loftpublications.com
www.loftpublications.com

If you would like to suggest projects for inclusion in our next volumes, please e-mail details to us at:
loft@loftpublications.com

Introduction

Seismology and seismic engineering are the two key fields involved in the analysis of earthquake phenomena. The former examines the subject from the standpoint of the earth sciences, that is, those dealing with the interior of our planet; the latter is oriented toward mitigating the dangers of earthquakes. There is, of course, a presupposition of an essential connection between the two fields.

Seismic engineering is a product of the 20th century, and its benchmarks are the 1906 San Francisco earthquake and the 1923 Kanto earthquake in Tokyo. However, the birth of modern seismology goes back to 1880 when the Japanese Seismology Society was created after the disastrous earthquake that hit Yokohama.. Since then, the continuous accumulation of information about our planet, such as the determination of its interior structure, the discovery of its cooling processes, and the formulation of Wegener's theory on the origin of the continents, has been vital to an understanding of what takes place when the ground shakes beneath our feet.

Earthquakes are tremors in the terrestrial crust, products of a sudden freeing of mechanical energy. They originate in a prior accumulation of energy in the subsoil and are propagated in the form of waves. These movements provoke a series of vibrations that shake the crust, often giving rise to fissuring. They are considered one of the most traumatic of natural phenomena because in only a matter of seconds, often with no prior warning, they can cause an extremely high amount of devastation. It is estimated that during the 20th century the number of earthquake victims reached 50 million.

The main problem with earthquakes is the nonlinear nature of the many factors influencing their generation. This makes it practically impossible to predict the time and place of the next tremor. Thus, the only possible response to the ongoing seismic menace lies in the advancement of seismic engineering. The psychological, social, and economic implications of earthquakes also mean that this is a concern shared by the whole community. But of course it especially involves seismologists, geologists, geophysicists, architects, structural engineers, urban planners, economists, and insurance companies.

Advances in seismic engineering depend largely on the ability to observe and analyze the effects large terrestrial movements have on existing building structures. These point to construction defects such as calculation errors, poor building techniques, lack of inspection, and problems with materials.

The commonly accepted seismic design criteria focus on avoiding building collapse in high-intensity earthquakes (i. e.,on the Mercalli scale of I to XII, those greater than intensity

VII). However, these are being questioned in the more economically developed countries, where demands are being made to avoid not only collapse but also non-structural damage. Obviously, the main drawback of this new goal is that it tends to add to construction costs.

From the beginning, an important factor was whether the most suitable structural system is flexible (ductile) or rigid (walls). Recent research has generated new ideas about protection from seismic danger. One solution which is being advocated involves curbing the effects of tremors on structures through a mechanical system that absorbs part of the seismic energy reaching the building.

The Earth has three important seismic zones: the circum-Pacific belt, which includes the Pacific coast from Chile to Alaska as well as many Asiatic islands such as Japan, the Philippines, New Guinea, and New Zealand; the trans-Asiatic (Alpide), which passes through the Himalayas, Iran, Turkey, the Mediterranean, and southern Spain; and the belt situated in the center of the Atlantic Ocean (the submerged mid-Atlantic Ridge). Some 81% of the largest earthquakes that have occurred were in the circum-Pacific belt, and 17% were in the trans-Asiatic belt.

This book is organized like a tour, following the paths of the main seismic regions. We begin in the trans-Asiatic belt (Spain, France, Turkey), then proceed to the circum-Pacific (New Zealand, Chile, Nicaragua, Mexico, the United States, Japan, and China).

The 25 projects described have in common a relationship to seismic events, from buildings that have experienced earthquakes in the design, construction, or use phase to those that are in zones of some (or even great) seismic risk which must, therefore, meet existing earthquake standards. There are others that must continue to perform after earthquakes have hit, emergency dwellings for people who are homeless after the ground stops shaking. There are also buildings which, because of their enormous height, pose a challenge to conventional seismic design. All in all, it is a multifaceted view that offers anyone with a minimal amount of curiosity a first glimpse of a world both terrible and fascinating.

The need to prepare ourselves—physically and psychologically—for something as inevitable and unpredictable as an earthquake reminds us that in confronting nature's power the one thing which we must keep sight of is the profound respect we owe it. The phenomena in this book show the magnitude of our obligation.

Global Seismic Hazard Map

Produced by the Global Seismic Hazard Assessment Program (GSHAP), a demonstration project of the UN/International Decade of Natural Disaster Reduction, conducted by the International Lithosphere Program.

Seismic hazard is defined as the probable level of ground shaking associated with the recurrence of earthquakes. The assessment of seismic hazard is the first step in the evaluation of seismic risk, obtained by combining the seismic hazard with vulnerability factors (type, value and age of buildings and infrastructures, population density, land use, date and time of the day). Frequent, large earthquakes in remote areas result in high seismic hazard but pose no risk; on the contrary, moderate earthquakes in densely populated areas entail small hazard but high risk.

Seismic hazard maps depict the levels of chosen ground motions that likely will, or will not, be exceeded in specified exposure times. Hazard assessment programs commonly specify a 10% chance of exceedance (90% chance of non-exceedance) of some ground motion parameter for an exposure time of 50 years, corresponding to a return period of 475 years. The Global Seismic Hazard Map depicts peak ground acceleration (pga) with a 10% chance of exceedance in 50 years, given in units of m/s^2. The site classification is rock everywhere except Canada and the United States, which assume rock/firm soil site conditions. pga, a short-period ground motion parameter that is proportional to force, is the most commonly mapped ground motion parameter because current building codes that include seismic provisions specify the horizontal force a building should be able to withstand during an earthquake. Short-period ground motions affect short-period structures (e.g. one-to-three story buildings, the largest class of structures in the world). The map colors chosen to delineate the hazard roughly correspond to the actual level of the hazard. The cooler colors represent lower hazard while the warmer colors

Global map assembled by Domenico Giardini (ETH, Zurich), Gottfried Grünthal (GFZ, Potsdam), Kaye M. Shedlock (USGS, Golden), and Peizhen Zhang (CSB, Beijing). 1999

represent higher hazard. Specifically, white and green correspond to low hazard (0%-8% g, where g equals the acceleration of gravity, which is approximately 9.8 m/s^2); yellow and orange correspond to moderate hazard (8%-24% g); pink and dark pink correspond to high hazard (24%-40% g); and red and brown correspond to very high hazard (=40% g). In general, the largest seismic hazard values in the world occur in areas that have been, or are likely to be, the sites of the largest plate boundary earthquakes.

The Global Seismic Hazard Map and all associated documentation, including regional reports, maps of seismicity, source characterization information, and yearly GSHAP reports are available via the Internet through the GSHAP homepage, http://seismo.ethz.ch/GSHAP/. The GSHAP was designed to promote a regionally coordinated, homogeneous approach to seismic hazard evaluation and to provide the first quantitative global seismic hazard map. The GSHAP map and webpage are designed to assist in global risk mitigation through improved national and regional assessments of seismic hazard. The GSH map and reports may be used by national and regional agencies, decision makers, engineers, planners, emergency response organizations, builders, and the general public, for land use planning and improved building design and construction. Furthermore, the data and methods used to create the GSH Map may be used by national or regional agencies for further detailed studies applicable to their needs, especially more detailed seismic hazard maps.

Kaye M. Shedlock

Prefaces

Lebbeus Woods
A post-biblical view

Tadao Ando
Urban reconstruction throught greenification

Javier Pioz
Reflections on the action of earthquakes
on buildings

Llopis–Jiménez
Thoughts on practical application of the earthquake
resistance code

Lebbeus Woods

A post-biblical view

Earthquakes are the result of natural, tectonic changes in the solid crust of the earth and, as such, are not inherently catastrophic. Their bad reputation comes from the destruction to human settlements that accompanies them, when buildings collapse under the stress of forces produced by earthquakes. This destruction is not the 'fault' of earthquakes, but rather of the buildings, which, even in regions regularly visited by earthquakes, are not designed to work harmoniously with the violent forces periodically released. So buildings collapse, usually with considerable loss of life and injuries. Earthquakes are blamed, as though the purpose of these sublimely unself-conscious phenomena was to damage and destroy the human. "Earthquake Kills Thousands!" "Killer Quake Strikes!" "Earthquake Levels Town!" are typical aftermath headlines. What they should say is "Falling Buildings Kill Thousands!" "Killer Buildings Strike!" "Inadequately Designed Town Leveled!"

Such headlines will not, of course, appear. If they did, architects, town planners, engineers, and the entire army of professionals responsible for the design, construction, and maintenance of the affected buildings would be called to account. If that were to happen, they would certainly implicate politicians, developers, banks and the entire army of private and public officials controlling what gets built and where, the financial/economic community that finds it more profitable to rebuild what has been destroyed than to commission the development of architectures that would work with earthquakes and thus survive them. If this profit-driven community was called to account by public outcry, it would almost certainly turn the blame back on the public itself. After all, corporations and government are under constant pressure to give the public what it wants, which today means the same products, the same lifestyles, the same buildings and types of buildings everywhere on the planet, regardless of the planet's extremely varied processes of transformation. If all these individuals and social institutions were held responsible for the destruction caused by earthquakes, then the public in earthquake regions would have no choice but to demand radical changes. But this would be an expensive revolution, one that all the interests involved could afford only at great cost to their reputations, knowledge and technical expertise—and to their present economic prosperity.

There is, however, a deeper structure of resistance to investing in the creation of new effective anti-seismic architectures and this is formed by the most venerable beliefs about the relationship between the human and natural worlds, considered to be essentially hostile. The "Man versus Nature" attitude begins in the creation stories of some of the world's dominant religions. Christianity, Judaism and Islam share the Biblical account of the expulsion of Adam and Eve from the Garden of Eden, which came as a result of their desire for self-knowledge and independence from the rest of the unself-aware, wholly interdependent world. Many philosophers in past epochs have rationalized this belief, but it was René Descartes who best codified it for the modern era. His philosophy postulates an essential duality of the world, comprised of the human and the divine, which cannot be bridged, at least by the human. Not coincidentally, he also invented a mathematical system—analytical geometry—that organized the spatial and temporal properties of the human domain with great efficacy. Cartesian logic and geometry offer a pragmatic usefulness that shows no signs of diminishing, more than three hundred years after their inception, and in spite of immense cultural and technological changes to the society they serve. But, while Cartesian thought and method succeeded in freeing science, and therefore technology, from the grip of religion per se, it maintained the adversarial Biblical relationship between the domain of the human and the realm of divine nature. Nowhere is its fragility in this regard more clearly demonstrated than in earthquake regions. There, the idea of the Cartesian "grid" as a symbol of rational efficiency and stability has been overturned (literally) by the nature of earthquake forces. And the civilizational cornerstone of human independence from Nature—a conceit, however transparent, that has propelled the notion of human progress—has been broken to bits. In light of the consistent failure of leading societies such as the United States and Japan to build effectively against earthquake, it is reasonable to reconsider the dominant philosophies, techniques and goals of building and urban design in earthquake regions.

At this writing, such a reconsideration by architects and planners has hardly begun. This book will no doubt summarize the most recent and salient efforts to go beyond the defensive "reinforcement" of existing conceptual and physical structures, and open up genuinely new possibilities for architecture in relation to the earth's continuing process of transformation. My own efforts in this direction have been sporadic and sketchy, resulting in two sets of highly speculative projects, which were published in my book of 1997, *Radical Reconstruction*. The San Francisco "houses" of 1995, completed after research at the Berkeley Engineering Library, propose architectures extending the forces of earthquake into the dynamics of private life and social change. The "terrain" projects of 1999, completed after the cycle of disastrous earthquakes that struck around the world last autumn, propose that architecture be considered as an integral part of landscapes undergoing regular seismic upheavals. Both sets of projects look forward to a post-biblical reconciliation of the human and the natural—through the creative transformation of architecture itself.

Lebbeus Woods

Tadao Ando

Urban reconstruction throught greenification

It has now been five years since the Great Hanshin-Awaji Earthquake. The area hit by the quake is one where I have built a number of buildings over the last 30 years. I visited this stricken area many times inmediately after the earthquake and, while all of the buildings I built survived, the overhead expressway collapsed, buildings were flattened and the very life of the town was lost. As I stood looking at once familiar corners of districts that were now mere ruins, the scenes of my youth now gone, the scenes of my life which I treasured deep down inside wiped out in a matter of seconds, I felt total despair.

At this unbelievable sight, I was left feeling that it would take no less than ten years to resurrect the area from such a state of devastation. However, reconstruction has come quicker than I thought and while, at least on the surface, the painful scars of this devastating earthquake are disappearing, I feel that the speed of this recovery is in fact creating a rather large and important problem.

Urban reconstruction is, in my view, not only a question of physical and functional recovery, but should never lose sight of the psychological aspects it also carries with it. Therefore, I proposed to the related authorities and individuals that a portion of the original structure of those buildings deemed to be of value architecturally be retained as part of the new building in order to preserve the city's memories. But social requirements in such devastating situations prioritize to economics and speed and my request has not been accepted. So industrialized housing and pre-fab office buildings are popping up all over the city. In the end, there will be no city focal point which can serve as a new foundation to uphold spirit.

In badly stricken areas, because of the advantages in terms of construction time and cost, it is natural that prefabricated houses are erected one after another. However, these rows of assembly-line homes literally kill the scenery. Urban functions may have been restored but scenery which can liven the human spirit will not be revived, no matter how long one waits. I wondered whether we couldn't have created an environment that both soothed our hearts and improved as time went by.

This is why I have initiated a campaign, borrowing on the virtue and strength of plants and trees, to restore the scenery in these stricken areas. The target is to plant some 250.000 trees throughout these areas. And, as a mutual asset for the people of the area, and through everyone's protection and nurturing during their growth, I believe that we can recreate our town and bring about the birth of a new and rejuvenated community.

Such living things leave to the children of the next generation irreplaceable assets, scenery which will remain of value to them. Through each small action and effort on the part of each individual, it is my hope that we will match the area as an interrelated and expanding sphere.

Tadao Ando

Green Network

ひょうごグリーンネットワーク

Javier Pioz

Reflections on the action of earthquakes on buildings

The Third IFHS Congress on large skyscrapers, where the Bionic Tower prototype was introduced, concluded that the number of piles used in the concrete superstructures of very tall skyscrapers and the number and density of such buildings in the modern megalopolis contribute to soil and substructure deterioration. Thus, although structures capable of maintaining stability and absorbing earthquake vibrations have been developed, excessive perforation of the ground produces cracks in the streets and leads to the collapse of buildings.

Recent earthquakes have shown how some buildings are completely destroyed and simply collapse, while others maintain their geometric configuration but fall over from the base or shift several yards from their original location. In the former, bad construction is at fault and independent elements, not being solidly and flexibly connected, break, split, or bend. In the latter, excessive structural rigidity, common in solid, massive buildings, breaks the concrete structure at ground level, and the building is destroyed.

The explanation is both simple and complex. Imagine yourself building a house of cards on a table. As long as there are no external movements, the structure remains balanced. We give the table a push, even a light one, all the cards are likely to come tumbling down. Now imagine setting an ordinary solid brick in a vertical position with its base firmly clamped to the table. A strong, fast blow to the table, like a karate chop, will lop the brick off at clamp level and bring it down. What the example of the house of cards demonstrates is defective construction with absolutely no seismic-resistant measures. The brick illustrates good construction but inappropriate seismic-resistant measures.

Let us now imagine that on our field of operations we vertically arrange several plastic trays of the type commonly used to hold papers and documents—in/out boxes. It is easy to show that, even if we push the table hard, the tray structure will only vibrate and oscillate, undergoing mild deformation but finally recovering its original stability. This is what a flexible building does.

Extending the idea, when earthquakes occur in areas with historic and modern buildings close together, we usually find that, despite the apparent rigidity of the historic structures, these are the ones that remain standing while the modern buildings may tend to collapse. In spite of the fact that most of these older buildings are made of large blocks of stone, a material hardly associated with flexibility, the construction is intrinsically highly elastic and earthquake resistant. How can we explain this curious paradox? Usually, the large stone blocks in these buildings are joined by very rudimentary mud mortar that is elastic by nature. Metaphorically speaking, it is as if the stones were seated on Plasticine. This simple system is what allows the energy produced by the earthquake to be absorbed by spreading (microfragmenting) the force lines to every block of stone in the building, thus dissipating the energy through tiny deformations in the connecting mortar.

Returning to the example of the house of cards, imagine now that, using chewing gum, we connect all the cards to each other and to the table. The construction will then be virtually indestructible against any bouncing to which we subject the table. These simple experiments demonstrate that the problem in fighting seismic effects is not merely a question of choosing the right materials, but also of paying a good deal of attention to connectives and articulation.

Obviously, a house of cards or an in/out box structure is in no way directly comparable to a building. The deformations these flexible models can absorb are much greater than those a large structure can deal with. We need, then, an additional mechanism that eliminates part of the earthquake energy before it affects the structure. Returning to our in/out box structure, let us now situate it inside a large silicone container. The effect now is to drastically reduce the forces impacting on the superstructure, because they become greatly weakened by deformation of the plastic material. Thus, the need for significant deformation for the sake of additional stability is also reduced. Conceptually, we could summarize by saying that, to guarantee seismic-resistant building stability, we need to develop two systems working in unison: a flexi-structure system and an overall plastic isolation system.

How can we find an effective practical solution that meets these needs? For bionic engineers and scientists, the answer would be easy: "Nature has already done it and done it better." The only difficulties lie in finding appropriate reference models in nature and supplying the right analytical interpretations and conclusions. One of the most powerful tools nature has at its disposal to solve resistance problems in live organisms is force microfragmentation. When a natural structure needs to absorb heavy doses of energy, it does not pile on large masses of resistant material. To the contrary, forces are dissipated by division

into thousands and thousands of interconnecting, resistant fibers. Fractal, chaotic structures made up of fibers and air attain resistance levels tens of times greater than those achieved by massively concentrating fibers of a single element. Studying the logic of force microfragmentation, which allows large structures like trees, and small ones like lions' teeth or citrus fruits to develop structural defense mechanisms against seismic, wind-generated, or impact forces, is what led to the design of Bionic Tower joint systems like the Capsule Flexible Structure, Multiradial Floating Concretework, and Plastic Anti-seismic Multifragmentation.

It is not a question of looking to nature for imitative, concrete, formal solutions. In general, we have to find multiple ways to solve the same problem. And these ways are available. Bionics employs a scientific research focus derived from biology and technics—not in the initial sense of biotechnics (the correlation between biology and technology), but from analyzing biological technology. This results in insights derived from ideas applicable to engineering and architecture. Nature's suggestions offer concepts like bionic vertical space, fractal geometry, chaos theory, zero points, holism, and others that are just beginning to be managed with precision. These are innovative theories that will define human habitats in the coming century.

Javier Pioz

Llopis-Jiménez

Thoughts on practical application of the earthquake resistance codes

The problem of risk. Seismic risk:

At the dawn of the 21st Century, we live in a world where risk plays a fundamental role. It is indisputable that, in essence, life is pure risk. The constant effort to maintain it is, in fact, a constant struggle against everything that makes its permanent loss a possibility.

The complexity of life in our civilization produces a continual confrontation with very different types of dangers, assumed collectively or individually, in proportion to the degree of sophistication defining human relations (and, thus, in direct proportion to a country's level of development).

In many cases, the scale and complexity of risks make long-term predictions difficult. In any event, mitigating their consequences is a difficult and costly task. In fact, the tendency in the insurance world is toward progressive concentration of energies and legislation of additional guarantees in confronting the effects of large-scale catastrophes with highly uncertain outcome. Determining risk coverage always entails a cold process of computation and analysis, which includes an evaluation of the mathematical probability of misfortune actually occurring, followed, of course, by the estimation of contractual costs. When dealing with great natural catastrophes, we are speaking of costs involving untold millions of dollars.

Earthquakes belong to this risk category because they are among the most destructive natural catastrophes in terms of victims and material losses. And they have the greatest impact because of the extreme duration-destruction ratio, which may unfortunately translate into very great damage in a matter of seconds. It has been estimated, for example, that total direct and indirect losses from a large seismic disturbance originating in Andalusia (one of the highest seismic risk zones in Spain) could reach $10,000,000 if the epicenter were in the city of Seville. And if some other Andalusian capital were affected, we would be dealing with amounts ranging from $750,000,000 to $1,750,000,000 in damage (Martín Martín, A.J. (1993): *Danger and seismic risk*, Granada, Instituto Andaluz de Geofísica).

Because our current state of knowledge does not allow us to predict these physical phenomena with any degree of certainty, government efforts must concentrate on prevention, ranging from R&D investments in geophysics, seismic engineering, and related sciences, to the adoption of special urban development measures or earthquake-resistant building codes. These and other complementary measures, in any event, are part of earthquake damage-prevention policy. The acceptable level of risk and the cost guarantees for the envisioned level of security must be planned in connection with this policy.

Eurocode 8: analysis of fundamental differences with NCSE-94

The Eurocodes are experimental European directives (ENV) that have been approved by the European Normalization Committee (CEN) for provisional application. After a certain time period, CEN members can raise objections and propose amendments. These are then reviewed and adapted for inclusion and periodic review as European standards (FN). Parallel maintenance of national standards with the experimental provisions is accepted even if the two are contradictory, provided they are approved as ENs. The Eurocodes are thus not mandatory, but they carry weight and are used in building projects with increasing frequency today, despite the fact that some sections currently in effect may be pending revision due to the development of more recent criteria and approaches.

EC-8, entitled "Ordinances for earthquake-resistant structures", includes the following:

Part 1.1. General rules, basic requirements, and approaches for inspection criteria applicable to buildings and civil works.

Part 1.2. General rules applicable to the earthquake resistance of building projects, structural analysis, security checks, and the effects of torsion, as well as suggested basic principles for project layout and formulas to estimate the life of buildings.

Part 1.3. Standards applicable to buildings with reference to materials and structural elements made of those materials.

Part 2. Rules for bridges.

Part 3. Rules for towers, derricks, and chimneys.

Part 4. Rules for large pipelines, tanks, and silos.

Part 5. Ordinances on geotechnical conditions, foundations, and retaining walls, applicable to building construction.

For greater clarity, we have divided the material covered by both documents in two main sections: foundations and superstructures.

Foundations:

First, it is important to emphasize that both NCSE-94 and EC-8 agree on rejecting the concomitance of both surface level foundations and deep substructures in supporting a single superstructure. Thus, both standards advocate the creation of joints in the super-structure, so it is clearly divided into independent units, when soil discontinuity requires.

The two standards also agree on the need to join surface foundation sections together with beams when predicted seismic magnitudes correspond to certain predetermined values. However, they differ with regard to the estimation of the amount of steel reinforcement in those components.

Regarding substructures, i.e. pile-structured foundations, NCSE-94 provides little information, unlike EC-8. The latter specifies the number of piles and takes into account not only the superstructure's gravitational force, but also the movements affecting the pile due to shaking of the soil. This is important when substructures are being placed in high seismic risk zones where there are massive plates notorious for changes in rigidity. EC-8 is rigorous in this area, whereas NCSE-94 is much less stringent. For example, with regard to reinforcement, NCSE-94 considers minimal steel reinforcement sufficient, both longitudinally and crosswise.

Structural considerations:

Limiting discussion to aspects considered of primary importance, first there is the procedure for calculating earthquake action. Both directives deal with macroanalysis: simplified methods and dynamic analysis for those structures that fail to meet the minimum requirements of structural simplicity stipulated by each standard. EC-8 views the problem in a much more basic manner than NCSE-94. The former studies earthquake actions in the first vibration mode, which means that the total building mass is equal to the effective mass of the mode considered. In terms of unlimited procedures due to conditioning morphologies, EC-8 deals with nonlinear analysis of temporal response, frequency analysis, and the stochastic analysis, which is not mentioned in NCSE-94.

Another very important aspect in earthquake resistance structural studies is relative lateral displacement, which involves the study of second order effects that may significantly influence overall superstructure stability, as well as related damage to adjacent constructions.

Finally, it is important to bear in mind the fragility and distortion of elements without structural support, which would suffer deformation and potential damage with displacement. In this regard, NCSE-94 proposes a simple equation in terms of the actual deformation potential of the structure, elastically and ductilely. EC-8 only considers the problem of the building when in use, addressing an earthquake with a shorter recurrence period.

There is also a very significant emphasis on structural behavior, in which both directives largely agree, with some exceptions: structural shape in relation to ground plan and building height symmetry, changes in height rigidity, and their distribution on the ground plan. This area deserves special attention in terms of seismic resistant behavior. Their influence is decisive in terms of matching the blueprint to the actual constructed piece.

Also important is the effect of torsion, covered in both documents. They agree on what is considered the minimum value: 5% of the transversal dimension on the plane the forces of inertia act on and which contains the crossbeams under study.

Finally, we should point out the important differences observed in the soils mentioned in the two regulations. Soil classification affects the elastic response spectrum, and this in turn influences the estimate of earthquake activity. Standardization of criteria between both documents on this point is thus highly important for the future.

The version of NCSE-94 currently in effect. Professional aims and implications:

When this document came into effect it resulted in a decided change in design and structural calculations of buildings in earthquake zones. In the comments on its issuance, the text states: "The final aim of these criteria is to avoid loss of human life and reduce the financial costs which future earthquakes may occasion." This involves limiting serious structural damage from earthquakes with an appreciable likelihood of their occurrence during the life of the building (about fifty years) and avoiding structural collapse in the event of a major earthquake (when the likelihood of occurrence is on the order of 10% during a building's life). This implies that the level of security, and thus the risk of damage, is within the framework of the directive's scientific criterion. It is indeed sufficient to achieve the primary aim, preserving human life, while more problematic in terms of the level of monetary savings implied for society as a whole. This last point demonstrates the great difficulty in precisely computing the security criteria, which correspond in the final instance to economic operations involved in the complex construction sector, both publicly and privately.

The problem lies in the impossibility of demonstrating in practice the effectiveness of the measures being adopted in order to justify their cost. It is this uncertainty that introduces a permanent tension when incorporating technical advances, not between the correct or the incorrect, but between what is sufficient and what is most sufficient. This entails special coordination between developers and qualified experts, who must come to an understanding when establishing risk hypotheses, assuming all of the concomitant responsibilities. This must all be understood in the context of a highly demanding society. But it is separate from the problem of the great number of variables qualified experts must take into account when making basic computational and earthquake-resistant design decisions.

This justifies the need to face the problems with professional rigor, carefully employing the regulation's legal requirements, and weighing the decisions that are at the discretion of the project's head. Adequate training of the experts in each field is thus fundamental in the construction process, although we are moving inexorably toward the specialization and interdisciplinary collaboration suitable to each situation. Passage of the Building Law will tend to clarify these issues as levels of responsibility are more precisely defined. They are, after all, the final authority supporting the insurance calculations of professionals and companies with regard to the risks to which we referred earlier.

Practical difficulties in applying the directive:

One of the main contributions of NCSE-94 is a definitive new earthquake map showing hazard areas based on likelihood of occurrence. This map is the basis of the fundamental seismic magnitude determination (for a recurrence period of 500 years) and of the contribution coefficient, parameters which establish the magnitude for computation purposes and which, in turn, provide the basis for subsequent mathematical analysis.

The situation has a serious negative effect on the computation coefficients and design requirements after a certain level of earthquake magnitude computation (normally for $a_c >$ 0.16 g). This has enormous impact on architecture and, when all is said and done, on the work of construction professionals.

To begin with, NCSE-94 requires that the necessary ductility of a structure be determined prior to proceeding with its computation. It also involves rating of normal or special significance. Both of these, obviously, have great economic impact. NCSE-94 also devotes an entire chapter to detailed design rules and building requirements in earthquake zones. The configuration of the building is covered, along with the arrangement of its mass, joints, structural systems, and non-structural elements. It also deals with conceptualization and design of substructures, and has an important series of determinations with regard to different structural types, including its general use and special fragility if subjected to stress produced by horizontal oscillations.

All of this is fundamental to architectural output. It is for all practical purposes impossible to discuss architectural design without mentioning structural design in the same breath, since this is what to the project's backbone. The early phases of all architectural work of any note must include basic insights regarding natural light, proportion, context, landscape adaptation, energy optimization, color, texture, and structural conception. But tectonics, which guarantees Vitruvian *firmitas*, is inescapable in any case and on any scale. This causes the requisite professional compromise of the architect who is aware of the service he or she provides to society.

From this perspective, it is easy to see how the regulations' design criteria straitjacket artistic freedom. Indeed, they affect the organization of shapes and volumes and, thus, control architecture's most elemental compositional resources. Any construction, whether new or a renovation, should adapt to the seven basic principles bearing the stamp of centuries of experience:

1. The principle of the symmetry of masses and rigidity.

2. The principle of harmony in dimensional proportion.

3. The principle of opposing gravity, which advocates lightness and a low center of gravity.

4. The principle of elasticity, employing resistant materials that behave uniformly.

5. The principle of substructure solidity, using compact and sufficiently rigid solutions which are as ductile as possible.

6. The principle of a closed perimeter using vertical and horizontal frames and borders.

7. The principle of insulating movement, using concepts and devices that permit mini-

mum impact when the building is subjected to oscillation.

The intention is to search for the greatest structural order possible in the work's design and to implement good building practices with proven results, whether mandatory or just recommended. This does not mean additional costs, although it does require additional project control efforts.

In other cases, however, there are economic repercussions. For example when concrete is used, the reinforcement adds to the expense (because of the amount used, increased anchorage length, increased number of braces, or increased complexity of lap and joint execution). The use of isolation beams or an increase in the size of columns may also be necessary. There is also a progressive increase in the technical aspects of the manufacture of building elements, especially bricks, stairways, facings and fine finishes, exterior carpentry, and installations.

In the next few years, the market will establish construction standards and superstructure types, with a foreseeable rise in metallic solutions to the detriment of reinforced concrete.

Finally, it is important to stress the great significance of soil. Problems caused by earthquakes, for example landslides, faults, cracks, liquefaction, and focused topographical effects, cannot be underestimated in deciding where to build in relation to terrain type. It is thus absolutely essential to have adequate regional and urban planning, which is responsible for zoning, productive activities, and special risk installations. In certain cases, the convergence of topographic, geotechnical, and seismic factors may even suggest the classification of certain soils as inappropriate for urban development. The involvement of experts and local and regional governments is necessary in this regard.

In addition, the need to determine the nature of the topsoil cannot be ignored in connection with final decisions on the degree of ground-structure interaction in order to optimize a building's physical and mechanical response. This leads to the importance of geotechnical research, necessary on any scale of intervention if one is to have suitable working hypotheses.

In the case of the Polytechnic Center of the University of Granada, as will be seen in the next pages, many of the difficulties in interpreting and complying with the regulations we have explained here come together. The end result is a rigorous, contrasting exercise with the participation of a wide range of architects, engineers, technical architects, and their firms in the different project phases and the work. (Of course, there has been no trial by fire, i.e. a significant earthquake).

We would hope this essays contributes to the manifold panorama of international earthquake-resistant activity by adding thoughts developed from a respect for the basic security necessities that must be the goal of our work. It is, moreover, a clear example of the important role which public administration must play in the construction sector, adopting advanced technological solutions in prevention measures before seismic disasters occur.

The buildings in this book, chosen from among the most outstanding in the world, demonstrate different ways to approach the problem of earthquakes. Some buildings, on high-risk sites, have even suffered the ordeal of an earthquake. With their diverse provenances and uses, they present a widely varied panorama. They require careful reflection in order to understand the theoretical and practical contribution each makes. All are serious and hopeful efforts to overcome the difficulties we encounter in adapting to nature's excesses.

Luis Llopis García
Manuel Jiménez

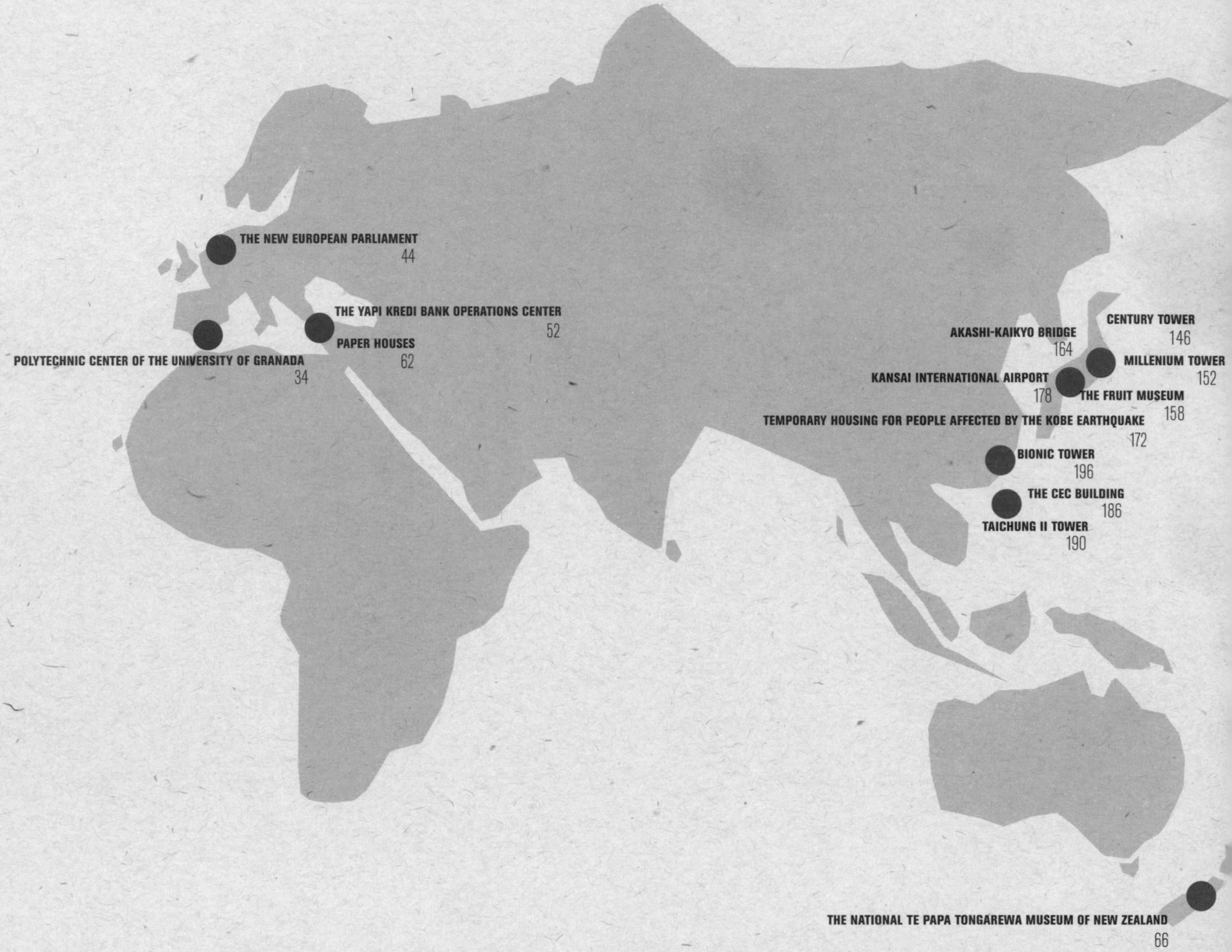

THE NEW EUROPEAN PARLIAMENT
44

THE YAPI KREDI BANK OPERATIONS CENTER
52

PAPER HOUSES
62

POLYTECHNIC CENTER OF THE UNIVERSITY OF GRANADA
34

CENTURY TOWER
146

AKASHI-KAIKYO BRIDGE
164

MILLENIUM TOWER
152

KANSAI INTERNATIONAL AIRPORT
178

THE FRUIT MUSEUM
158

TEMPORARY HOUSING FOR PEOPLE AFFECTED BY THE KOBE EARTHQUAKE
172

BIONIC TOWER
196

THE CEC BUILDING
186

TAICHUNG II TOWER
190

THE NATIONAL TE PAPA TONGAREWA MUSEUM OF NEW ZEALAND
66

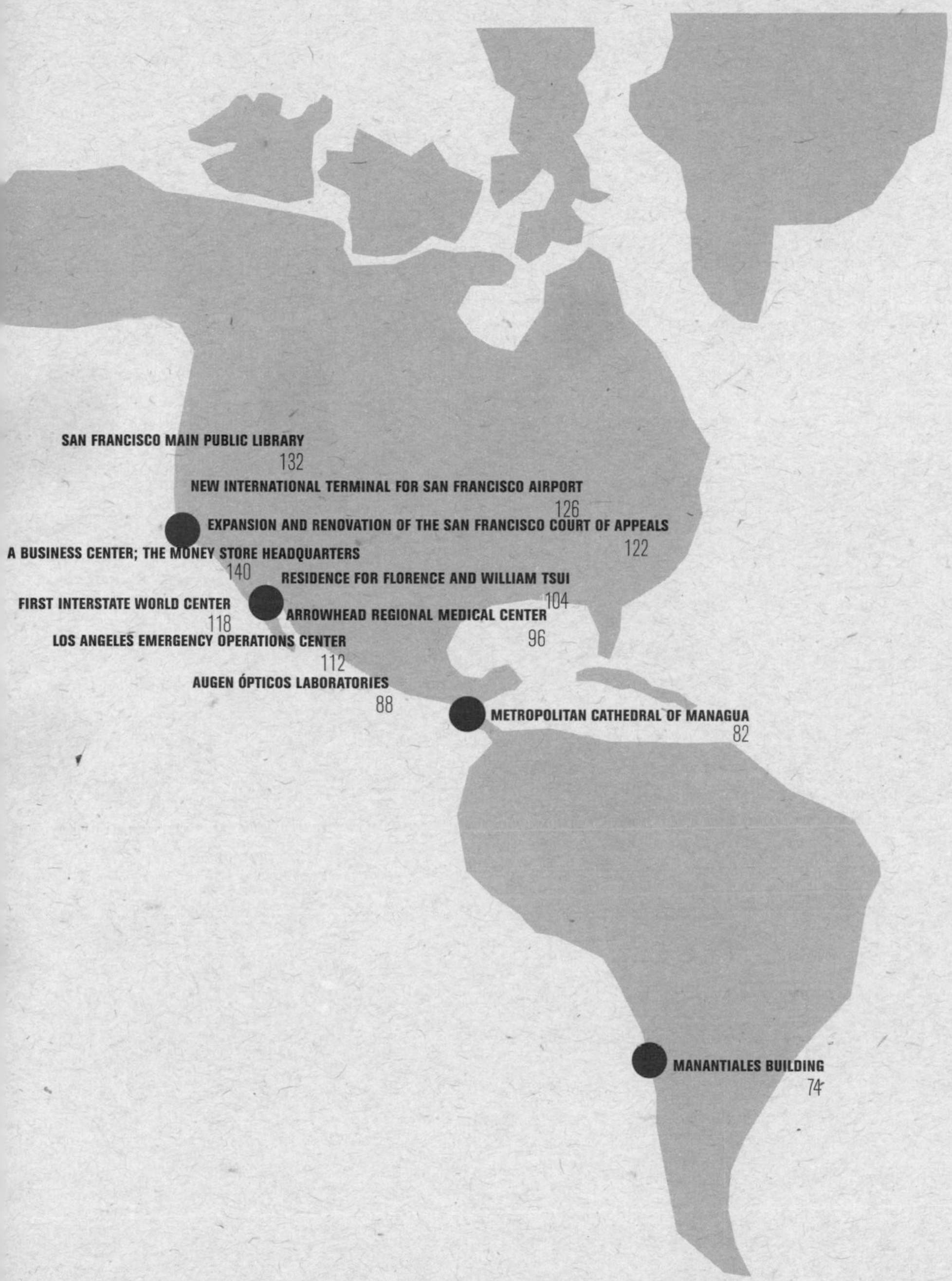

SAN FRANCISCO MAIN PUBLIC LIBRARY
132

NEW INTERNATIONAL TERMINAL FOR SAN FRANCISCO AIRPORT
126

EXPANSION AND RENOVATION OF THE SAN FRANCISCO COURT OF APPEALS
122

A BUSINESS CENTER; THE MONEY STORE HEADQUARTERS
140

RESIDENCE FOR FLORENCE AND WILLIAM TSUI
104

FIRST INTERSTATE WORLD CENTER
118   ARROWHEAD REGIONAL MEDICAL CENTER
96

LOS ANGELES EMERGENCY OPERATIONS CENTER
112

AUGEN ÓPTICOS LABORATORIES
88

METROPOLITAN CATHEDRAL OF MANAGUA
82

MANANTIALES BUILDING
74

EARTHQUAKE ARCHITECTURE

New construction techniques for earthquake disaster prevention

M.A. Graciani, Llopis Architects
and J.E. Martínez de Angulo

POLYTECHNIC CENTER OF THE UNIVERSITY OF GRANADA

The virtue of symmetry

Location **Fuentenueva Campus in University of Granada, Granada, Spain** Construction period **1998-2000** Clients **Regional government of Andalusia and the University of Granada** Foundations and structure **Edelmiro Rua Rodríguez, José María Rodríguez Ortiz, Manuel Jiménez Domínguez, Oficina Técnica Huarte SA (OHL), Asistencia Técnica Cotas Internacional SA** Works management **José Antonio Llopis Solbes, Luis Llopis García, Manuel Jiménez Domínguez and Cotas Internacional SA** Coordination of safety and health **Cristina Llopis García** Photographs **Manuel Jiménez Domínguez and Estudio Llopis**

Spanish standard to be met **NCSE-94**
Horizontal ground acceleration **0.24**
Expected period between earthquakes **500 years**

Area of plot **2.6 acres**
Surface area of complex **36,600 sq. ft.**
Total floor space constructed **245,400 sq. ft.**
Number of floors **9 (1 of them below ground level)**
Measurements of the standard floor **186 x 186 feet**
Height above ground **108 ft.**
Distance embedded into the ground **18 ft.**
Total cost **11,000,000 (as of March 2000)**

the Polytechnic Center of the University of Granada, with a powerful, prismatic exterior covered in white concrete, accommodates all the complex functions of a university of this standing and character.

The building, highly visible in the absence of nearby structures, is in the center of a trapezoid-shaped 2.6 acre plot. The ground floor is surrounded by a wide interior roadway which sets it apart from the surrounding campus. There are three floors below the natural grade and six above. The main entrance is through two impressive pedestrian passageways which link the first floor above grade with the university avenues. These outside areas are connected to the interior roadway by a vehicle ramp, open staircases, and a remarkable helical ramp. The complex occupies 36,600 square feet of the plot, with the remaining 76,400 square feet developed and landscaped.

All programs and university activities are carried out in the 245,400 square feet of floor space in the building. The various floors accommodate different functions based on program needs and relationships. The lecture halls, classrooms, and other teaching areas are organized around a cylindrical space illuminated from above by a pyramidal skylight atop a parallele-piped cornice. This open space connects each floor, providing atmosphere and distributing the natural light throughout. The floors are designed around four communication nuclei containing the covered staircases, four high-capacity elevators, rest rooms, and the vertical system shafts.

Due to its location on the Spanish seismic danger map, the building has been given a horizontal ground acceleration value of 0.24 (basic seismic acceleration in relation to the acceleration of gravity) with an earthquake expected every five hundred years.

Given the importance of the building, and bearing in mind the seismic conditions, from the outset the structural model was based on a very simple morphology, so its actual behavior during an earthquake would be very similar to predictions drawn from the analysis of forces on the model.

The structure is a prism with a 186 foot by 186 foot base, measuring 108 feet from ground level to the top of the cornice. The building goes 18 feet below ground level. These proportions were adopted in the expectation that they would not give rise to twisting or slippage. Stability is increased since the building is partly underground as it creates potential passive pressure mobilization in the extrados of the basement walls.

The total mass of each floor is not significantly different. Extra weight is uniformly distributed around the floor's center of rigidity, thus minimizing potential twisting caused by a seismic tremor. With this distribution of mass, the structural analysis only took into account the minimum eccentricity between the center of mass and the center of rigidity established according to the standards.

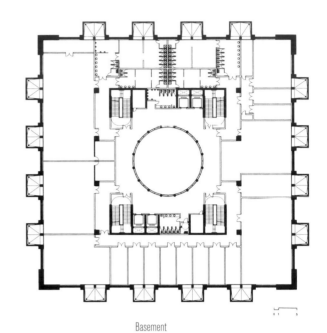

Basement

Granada as seen from the Polytechnic Center and three general views of the building

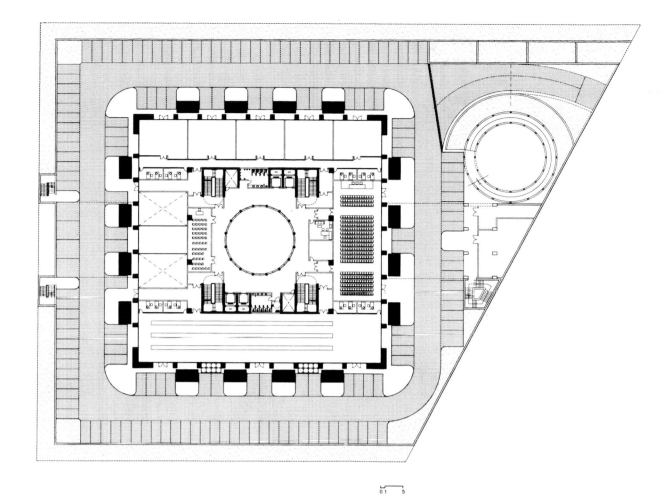

Ground floor, general plan: Laboratories, seminary rooms and meeting rooms

Top: A general view of the two structures that make up the Polytechnic center: the square based prism and the helical ramp. Bottom: The helical pedestrian ramp seen from above.

Right: The vehicle access ramp and parking area around the perimeter

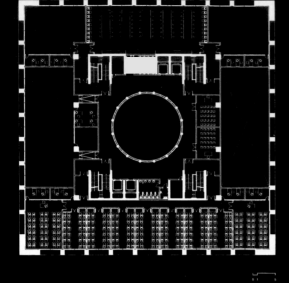

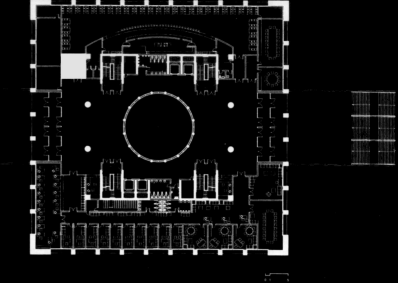

Mezzanine floor. Computer department, data processing center, and laboratories

Street level. Reception, administration, management, café, and document reproduction

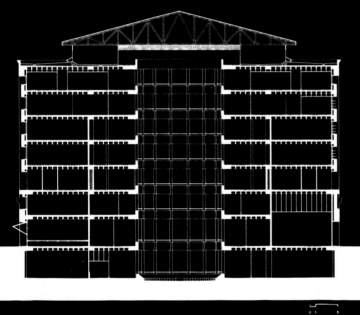

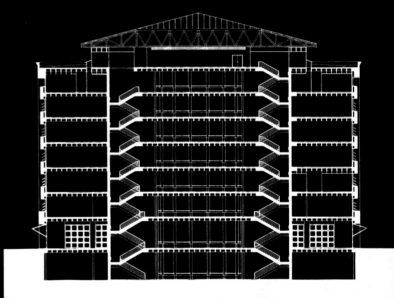

Section through the central space

Section through the stairwells

General view of the main lobby at street level. On the left and right are the entrances to the stairwells, running within the reinforced concrete walls all the way up the building. These stairwells are pressurized for ventilation and to prevent smoke accumulation in case of fire. On the right, the central courtyard which spatially connects all the floors

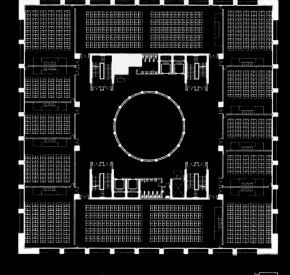
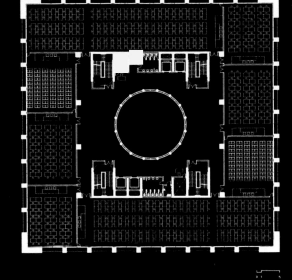

First and second floors above street level. Classrooms for theory classes

South elevation

North elevation

Classroom for theory classes, with natural light from large windows. To avoid the effect from short columns, the ledges on the exterior are independent of the supports, creating open interfaces

Installing building systems and wiring on the top floor. The 590 ft. beam that crowns the facade and forms the window lintels can be seen on the left. The windowsills are prefabricated, reinforced white concrete, flexibly joined to the columns

It was eventually decided that the interior walls on the top floor would be double plasterboard, sound-proofed with fiberglass. It is a very light system which will permit great flexibility of layout in the future

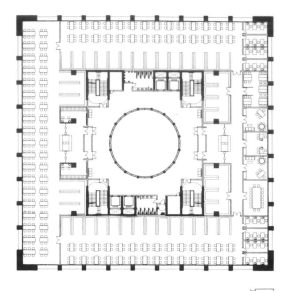

Third floor: The library

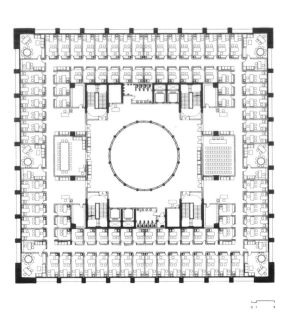

Top floor: Professors' offices and meeting rooms

The grid for each floor was executed in four parts, specially assembled to minimize the retraction problem. However, as there are no structural joints, a double symmetry is guaranteed. The greater isotropy reduces torsion forces to the minimum throughout the building

Detail of the metal grid structure for the concrete

August 1998

September 1998

November 1998

The two building-access walkways were designed with freestanding joints and supports so they would be independent from the building, because the different types of vibration could reduce their effectiveness as an evacuation route during an earthquake

January 1999

Close-up of the neoprene supports for the walkways

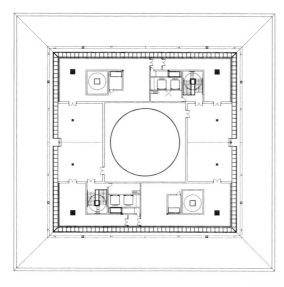

The attic: Building systems

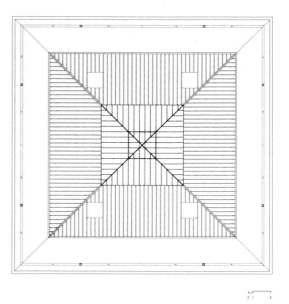

The roof

Detail of the intermediate column grid structure

The potential for ground/structure resonance was avoided by designing a structure with a very short vibration period compared to the vibration period of the ground, which is likely to be long. This was achieved by placing a very rigid, resistant framework without structural joints over thick flagstones, and with a ground floor surrounded by walls and set into the ground. Another factor adds even more stability: the geometric layout of the interior divisions of the space and resistant elements provide a double symmetry with respect to the orthogonal axes, the original coordinates of which go through the building floor's center of gravity

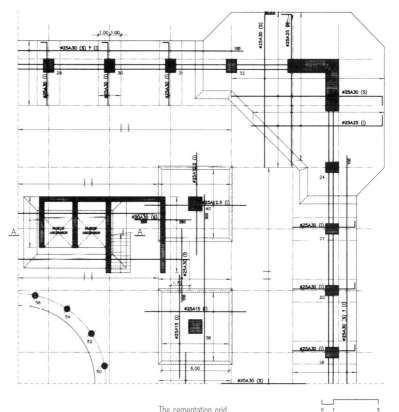

The cementation grid

Partial view of the cementation grid

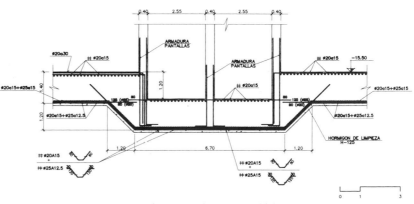

Cross section of cementation grid A-A

Different phases in the construction of earthquake-resistant baffles on the corners of the building: grid, forms, and two views of the final result

Resistance to horizontal movements comes from highly rigid elements placed orthogonally on the exterior. This is reinforced by the symmetrical configuration. Using the stairwells, elevator shafts and ductwork, very rigid elements employing reinforced concrete were put in place, so the center of gyration coincides almost exactly with the center of the building. The rigidity of these elements does not vary greatly with the building height. The stairwells were designed to be especially resistant and ductile so they could be used to escape during an intense earthquake

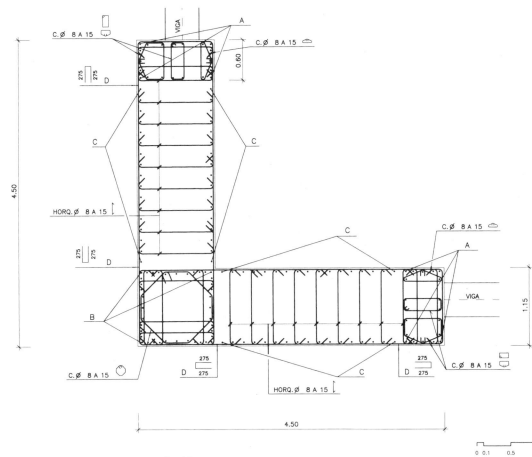

Armed floor

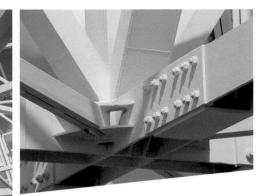

Partial views of the central axis which joins the roof trusses. This complex feature guarantees the necessary rigidity in a structure of this height. The joints are laminated steel reinforced with prestressed bolts

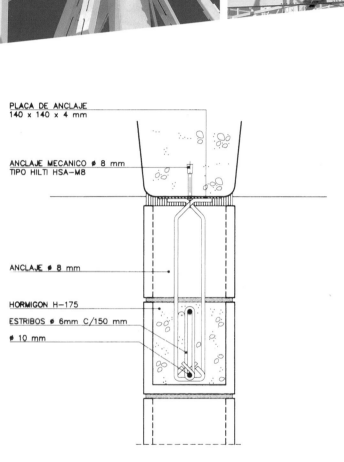

PLACA DE ANCLAJE
140 x 140 x 4 mm

ANCLAJE MECANICO ∅ 8 mm
TIPO HILTI HSA-M8

ANCLAJE ∅ 8 mm

HORMIGON H-175

ESTRIBOS ∅ 6mm C/150 mm

∅ 10 mm

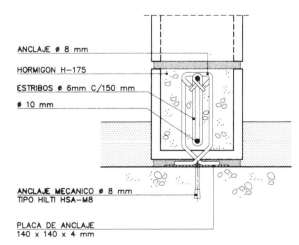

ANCLAJE ∅ 8 mm

HORMIGON H-175

ESTRIBOS ∅ 6mm C/150 mm

∅ 10 mm

ANCLAJE MECANICO ∅ 8 mm
TIPO HILTI HSA-M8

PLACA DE ANCLAJE
140 x 140 x 4 mm

Detail of the upper and lower bands that reinforce the interior concrete block partitions

The interior partitions have been designed so that they do add rigidity or resistance to the behavior of the structure during an earthquake. The aim was not to alter the center of rigidity once the resistance of the interior walls, normally connected to the structure, has been overcome. Accordingly, the internal walls have flexible seams, not fixed rigidly to the frame of the floor but sealed with an elastic material

Architecture Studio

THE NEW EUROPEAN PARLIAMENT

A great transparent mass

Associated architects **Atelier d'Architecture Gaston Valente** Location **Strasbourg, France** Construction period **1991-1999** Client **S.E.R.S.** Construction company **G.P.C.I.** Technical design **Sogelerg, Ote, Serue, Etf** Technical control **Socotec, Veritas, Cep** Photos **George Fessy** Aerial photos **Airdiaso**

Seismic risk **Category of Strasbourg according to the measurement scale used in France, zones are designated as 0, Ia, Ib, II and III (the latter being the highest seismic risk). The Strasbourg area is classified Ib, medium seismic risk**
Importance of the seismic design of the European Parliament **High because the chamber in which the European Union deliberates is a vital building**

Total floor space **2,368,000 sq. ft.**
Number of floors **17 above ground level, 3 below**
Diameter of the tower **328 ft.**
Height of tower **197 ft.**
Total number of offices **1,133**
Surface area of main façade **139,900 sq. ft.**
Surface area of roof **157,700 sq. ft.**
Amount of concrete used **130,000 tons**
Amount of steel used **14,000 tons**
Total cost approximately **$3,000,000,000 (as of June 1998)**
Total cost per square foot **1,390 dollars**

General aerial view

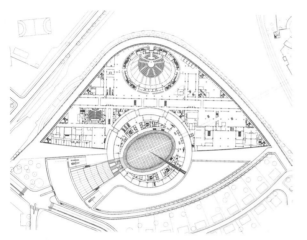

General plan (level +3.67)

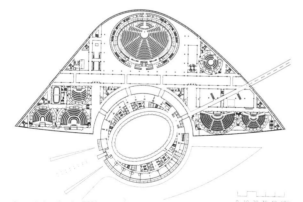

General plan (level +7.33)

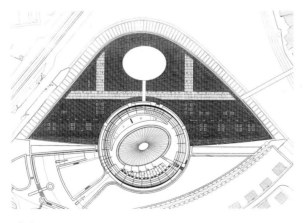

Roof

this building was commissioned after Strasbourg was officially named as the site of the European Parliament, although the city had been performing this function provisionally since 1958. The goal was a building which would employ the highest design and construction standards for both compositional and structural elements. It also needed to represent the European Union, embodying the concepts of democracy, freedom and peace and expressing strong but thoughtful and judicious power. After a worldwide competition, the design of the Gaston Valente team was chosen in recognition of the way they communicated these concepts without falling into the trap of the project, of oppressive, brutal architecture despite the enormous scale and complexity.

The site is northeast of the historic center of Strasbourg, where the River III joins the canal that leads to the Rhine. Flowing east in front of the European Commission buildings, the river forms a perfect 400-yard-long curve. To the west sits a garden city dating from the 1920s. Its orthogonal rows of identical little houses are surrounded by trees. In the distance, the spire of Strasbourg cathedral rises into the sky. Against this backdrop, the project, which occupies the entire 11-acre parcel, uniquely expresses the relationship between interior and exterior, between content and emptiness.

The European Parliament is easily recognized. Its three geometric shapes, the horizontal arch, tower, and dome, are eye-catching. But one unique structural framework - the arch- supports the entire building and functions in a different way for each of the three volumes.

The arch is supported by a cross structure, 31.5 ft. by 31.5 ft. Some columns are as high as 165 ft. The framework varies as it nears the façade and becomes thinner where it takes up the weight of the double glass skin, which surrounds the interior space and provides the desired transparency.

In a medium-risk seismic zone like Strasbourg, the monolithic design of the circular tower, with a fan of columns and a succession of concrete walls emanating from its center, is earthquake-resistant. Superimposed circles and ellipses provide spaces for staircases, elevators, and duct work.

The strength of reinforced concrete allowed the framework thickness to be reduced and the space between the pillars to be increased. Consequently, less concrete and steel were needed and there was a significant gain in flexibility and resistance, which are much greater than normal.

The building, with its 2,152,800 square feet of space, spread over 21 floors and visible from afar, exemplifies macroarchitecture. Still, while the European Parliament appears, from the outside, to be a unified whole, it is actually a combination of different planes, masses, and perspectives. The architectural dialogue reflects both the urban and human scales of the project.

Above: Arch

Below: Tower

Interior of the tower

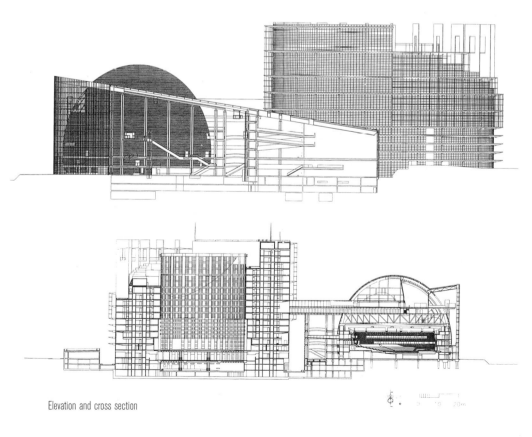

Elevation and cross section

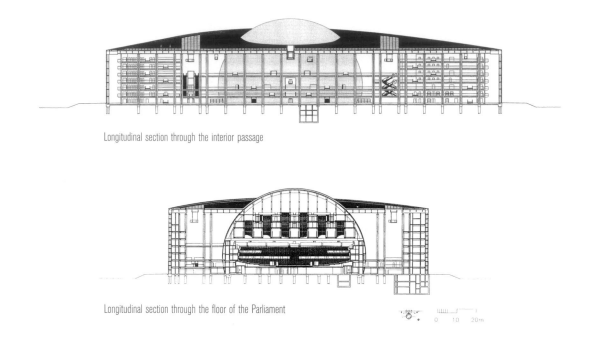

Longitudinal section through the interior passage

Longitudinal section through the floor of the Parliament

0 10 20m

Night view of the dome through the façade, with the tower in the background

The building is made up of three integrated forms: a horizontal arch, a dome and a tower, which encompass the different functions taking place inside.

The most emblematic part of the complex, the amphitheater, is the scene of the principal activity: deliberation. Its dome-shaped wooden shell emerges from the sloped roof like the prow of a ship against the river bank. The amphitheater seems to be positioned among the successive transparent layers of the arch like a suspended meteorite. Here, the conference halls, meeting rooms, and auditoriums necessary for the parliamentary sessions are located.

The dome's vertebrae-like arches rest on the concrete tambour while neoprene beneath the columns provides seismic elasticity and resistance

Right: Partial view of the dome from inside.
Bottom: Close-up of the cedar wood dome where it meets the sloping roof

Close-up of the interior façade

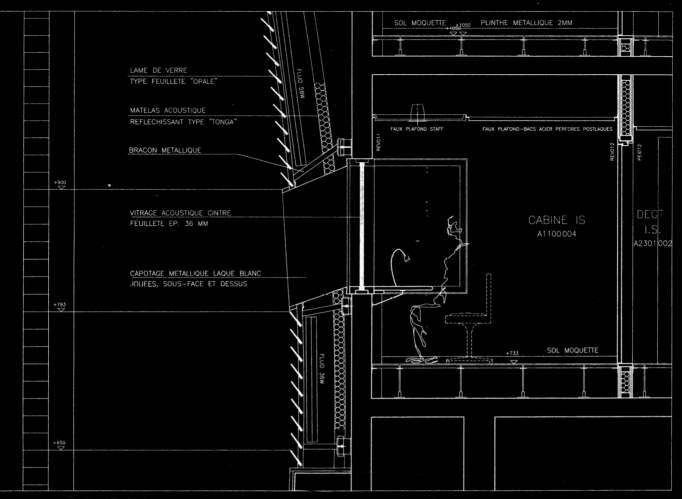

LAME DE VERRE
TYPE FEUILLETE "OPALE"

MATELAS ACOUSTIQUE
REFLECHISSANT TYPE "TONGA"

BRACON METALLIQUE

VITRAGE ACOUSTIQUE CINTRE
FEUILLETE EP. 36 MM

CAPOTAGE METALLIQUE LAQUE BLANC
JOUEES, SOUS-FACE ET DESSUS

+900

+783

+650

FLUO 58W

FLUO 36W

SOL MOQUETTE   PLINTHE METALLIQUE 2MM
+1050
+1050

FAUX PLAFOND STAFF   FAUX PLAFOND-BACS ACIER PERFORES POSTLAQUES

REVO11   REVO12   PEO12

CABINE IS
A1100004

DEG
I.S.
A2301002

+733   SOL MOQUETTE

Cross-section of the façade along one of the offices

The outer façade is comprised of glass panels joined with
flexible stainless steel clasps which double as shock
absorbers when there is any seismic movement. Each panel
can vibrate independently. Constructing and installing the
glass and the supporting infrastructure required an extremely
precise assembly process, systematically controlled by the
builders and designers

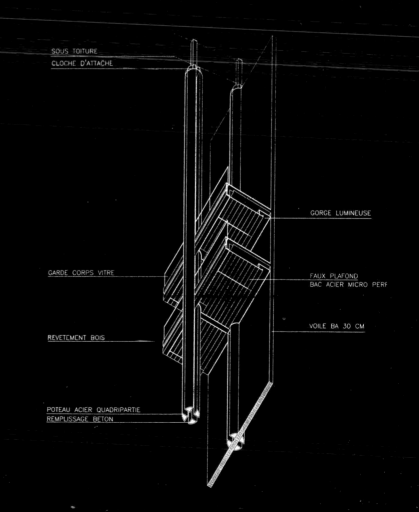

SOUS TOITURE
CLOCHE D'ATTACHE

GORGE LUMINEUSE

GARDE CORPS VITRE

FAUX PLAFOND
BAC ACIER MICRO PERF

VOILE BA 30 CM

REVETEMENT BOIS

POTEAU ACIER QUADRIPARTIE
REMPLISSAGE BETON

John McAslan & Partners

THE YAPI KREDI BANK OPERATIONS CENTER

Maximum efficiency

Associated Architects **Metex Design Group (Istanbul)** Location **Gebze, Turkey** Construction period **1993-1998** Engineers **Ove Arup & Partners** Façades **Arup Façade Engineering (AFE), Çuhadaroglu** Textile membrane **Koch Hightex GmbH** Interior designers **Tabanlioglu Architects** Furniture **Ahrend** Landscape gardeners **Peter Walker and Partners** Photos **Peter Cook/VIEW, Martin Hall and John McAsland & Partners**

Earthquake history **Two, both in 1999**
Earthquake damage **Only two broken windows**
Seismic risk **Level 4, a high risk zone**
Seismic design **In a massive earthquake, foreseen every 500 years, the design will prevent the total collapse of the framework. In a small tremor, there will be no structural damage**

Location **31 miles southeast of Istanbul**
Plot dimensions **2,100 sq. ft.**
Plot measurements **1,804 by 1476 feet**
Maximum height of the plot **653 ft. above sea level, to the east**
Minimum height of the plot **459 ft. above sea level, to the west**
Gross building area **495,000 sq. ft.**
Building capacity approximately **1,500 employees**
Office floor capacity **120 to 130 employees**
Space per employee **113 sq. ft.**
Surface area of the façade **193,750 sq. ft.**
Size of the park surrounding the building **1,800 sq. ft.**

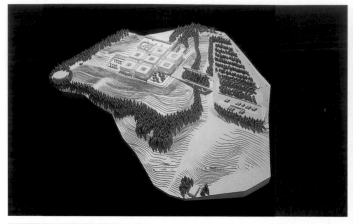

Top: Model of the site

Bottom: General view of the entire project

Right: The main entrance to the Operations Center

The operations center seats on top of a hill, taking advantage of the sea views and the natural setting. For security reasons, it has only three approaches. The main entrance, conspicuous due to its canopy, is used by employees and visitors. There is also a helipad and a delivery entrance for shipments

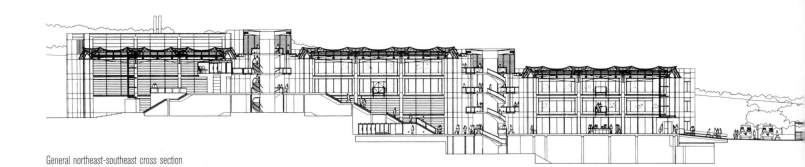

General northeast-southeast cross section

On the outskirts of the town of Gebze, atop a hill that runs down to the Sea of Marmara, the Operations Center built by the powerful financial group Yapi Kredi includes a computer center, training department, and other offices. The building design had to meet the client's requirements, the foremost being the construction of a safe building–it is in zone four, high seismic risk–without compromising on flexibility. It had to be able to adapt to the changing needs of a firm which encourages staff interaction and promotes a harmonious work environment. In addition, the architectural quality had to reflect the prestige of the company.

The project's ten components, including two added during the design process, occupy three levels following the natural slope. However, all floors have the same amount of space. The structural layout, the result of detailed study, ensures that the center can be expanded indefinitely, guaranteeing adaptability and enhancing seismic resistance because, for the plan to work, each of the units has to be independent.

Indeed, the oscillations (up to 2.36 inches) of each component must be absorbed by shared interstices, covered with a textile membrane, located between the parallelepipedal units. The metal arches have double support points which cover these arcades and were specifically designed to compensate for the different movements of the building. In fact, the steel building skeleton, stairs, bridges over the main and delivery entrance passageways, and panel coverings were all designed to neutralize both horizontal and vertical movements.

The project featured the special collaboration of landscape gardener Peter Walker who, showing great sensitivity to the original beauty of the site, brought in 6,000 indigenous plants to reforest the area. The new park, with athletic fields and space for relaxation, needs daily rainfall of approximately 4 l/m^2 between April and September. The vegetation has also been used to differentiate the arcades from each other, to help visitors get their bearings inside the building.

The Yapi Kredi Bank Operations Center design meets the demands of the site and the needs of the company with an unusually insightful, uncompromising, constructive solution.

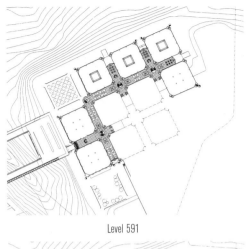

Level 591

Level 606

Level 619

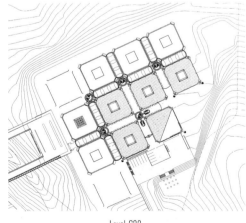

Level 632

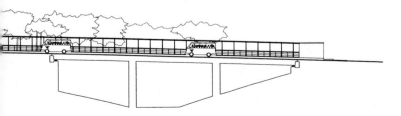

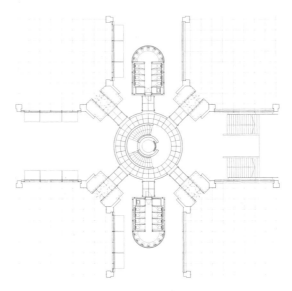

Front view and layout of the service
tower's floor-to-floor access

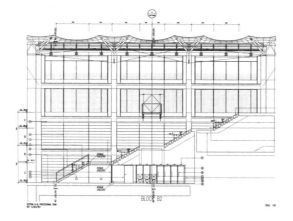

Front view and cross-section of an
arcade, seen from the stairs

View of an arcade from a service tower and
perspective of an arcade with the service tower in
the background

The foundations   The framework   Installing an arcade's covering

Above: A service tower under construction

Below: Erecting a stairway

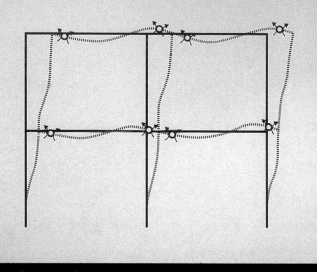

The Yapi Kredi Bank headquarters was designed to prevent any structural damage in the event of a low intensity earthquake. However, if a very strong, massive earthquake strikes, which might happen every 500 years or so, the plastic articulations in the beams will absorb the energy released during a tremor, preventing collapse of the framework. Seismic standards now routinely require this type of framework, in which beam flexibility is emphasized over column flexibility

Analysis of the response of the plastic articulations during an earthquake

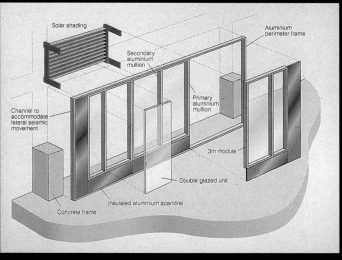

The installation of glass panels on the aluminum framework

The aluminum frames had to allow for variations in the concrete and the primary structure's capacity to absorb earth movement during seismic events. Sixteen columns on the perimeter and four on the interior patio absorb vertical forces. The stability of the columns comes from the exterior framework. The height of the columns varies between 14.76 feet at the entrance and 13.12 feet on the other floors

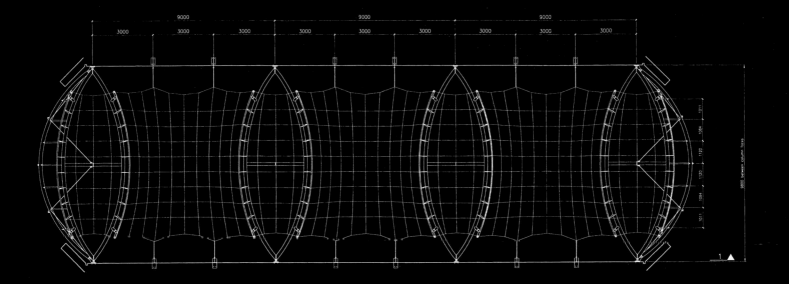

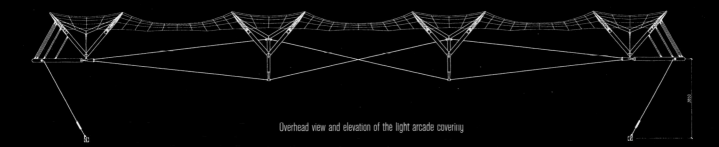

Overhead view and elevation of the light arcade covering

Each of the Center's ten components is structurally independent. Accordingly, the spaces between units, the arcades or internal streets, must absorb building oscillations of as much as 2.36 inches. The design of an earthquake-resistant system was thus focused on finding a type of covering that would tolerate these unequal displacements, without ramifications.

A metal framework with arches supported at two points was selected. Since the covering had to respond with great flexibility to any forces to which it is subjected, a textile membrane was considered the most appropriate solution. The glass of the walls enclosing the arcades also uses the metal framework of the covering to absorb building displacements without having to rely on expansion joints. The weight of the glass is supported by a curved beam, and the glass panels are joined by sealed articulations. Since building displacement from earthquakes can generate additional twisting forces, the elasticity of these joints prevents warping of the roof glazing

Close-up of the roof when completed (left) and while under construction (right)

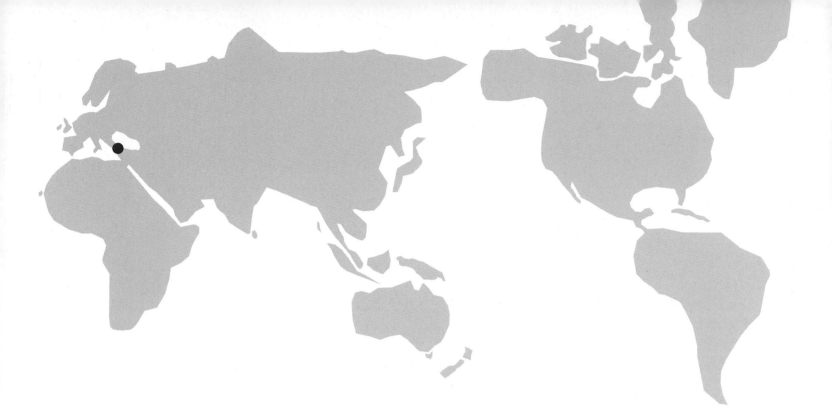

Shigeru Ban

PAPER HOUSES
An emergency dwelling for Turkey

Location **Bolu, Turkey** Construction date **1999-2000** Clients **Families left homeless after the earthquake** Photographs **Shigeru Ban**

Number of people who lost their homes during the
earthquake **Approximately 40,000**
Contributors **Local companies, Japanese construction
companies, the Istanbul Technical College and the
local nongovernmental organization, HSA, among
others**
Labor **Students and volunteers**

Gross building area **200 sq. ft.**
House dimensions **10 by 20 ft.**
Structure **Paper tubes**
Number of dwellings built (in December 1999) **17**

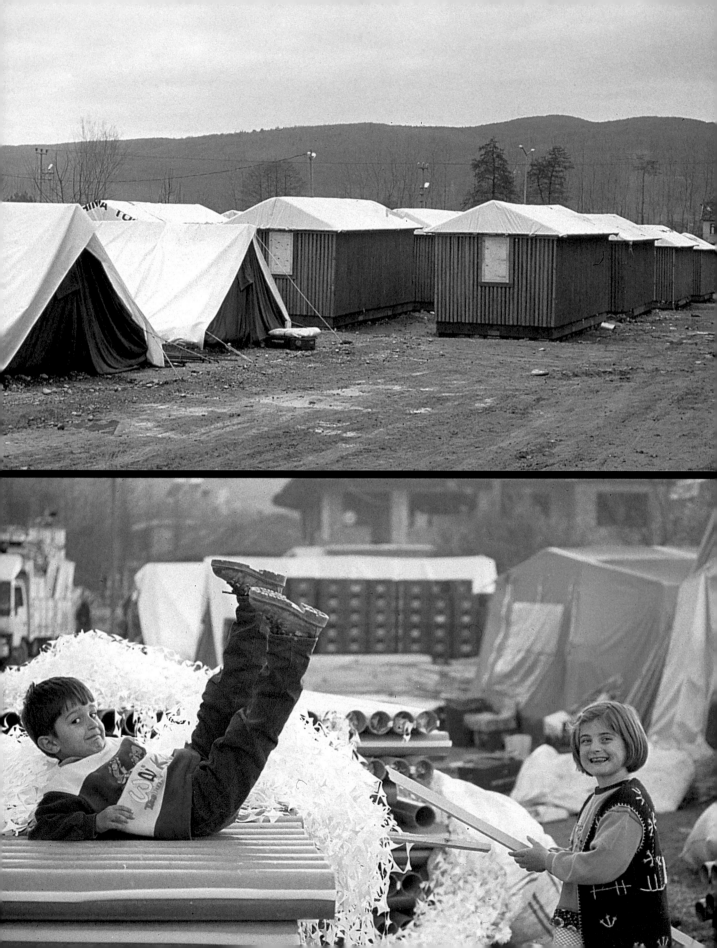

On November 12, 1999, an earthquake devastated Bolu, affecting 40,000 people. Many of them refused temporary shelters built by the Turkish government because they were too far from their workplaces, so Shigeru Ban gave the local residents the opportunity to build paper tube houses. The innovative material was first used in construction by the Japanese architect in the mid-1980s. It has advantages which make it ideal for use in emergency situations. In fact, it had first been tried in 1995, when the Hanshin Earthquake in Kobe, Japan, also left thousands of people homeless.

Paper tube construction provides, at minimal cost, a temporary dwelling that is more stable than the tents traditionally used in emergencies. It succeeds because it is available in a variety of thicknesses and sizes, and is durable, light, beautiful, and easy to make, transport, and install. It can be recycled after use and is easy to find in different parts of the world. Finally, it affords great overall comfort.

The paper tube house designed to meet living needs in Bolu was based on those previously constructed in Kobe. However, it was adapted to the climatic, social, and economic conditions present in Turkey. Thus, while a 13 ft. ground plan was used in Kobe, in Bolu the family size and standard wood lath dimensions favored a 10 by 20 ft. rectangle. Also, since Turkish winters are especially cold—much colder than those in Japan—the floors and roofs of the paper dwellings had to be insulated and the tubing had to be filled with waste-paper strips to increase their thermal inertia. Lastly, the sealing material used in Kobe was inadequate. In the end, cardboard and more sheeting material had to be used to provide acceptable insulation.

The entire process was made possible through the cooperation of various individuals and organizations from Turkey as well as from other countries. Local companies contributed paper tubes and beer crates for foundations. PVC sheeting material donated by Japanese construction companies served as construction material for Turkey and advertising for Japanese companies. Modules were prefabricated on the Istanbul Technical College campus and the building process was carried out (between classes!) by its students. A member of a local nongovernmental organization, HSA, coordinated the students and other volunteers who assembled the houses. Thus, through the combined efforts of many people from different walks of life, 17 houses were set up in December. Immediately people began to move in.

Previous page: General view of the camp.
Previous page bottom: Children playing with paper tubes and the paper strips that would go inside.
Above: Assembling the foundation and floor of a dwelling and installing the roof.
Below: Interior view of an occupied module

Not long before the Bolu earthquake, on August 17, another seismic event in the western Turkish city of Izmit killed more than 40,000 people and left a large part of the population homeless. At that time, Shigeru Ban began a campaign in Japan to get construction companies to donate as much PVC sheeting as possible to the homeless in Turkey. This would mean advertising for the Japanese, since the names of the companies appeared on the sheeting. For the Turks, it would mean improved living conditions, since it would replace less durable polythene or cotton material. A total of 643 sheets were collected and prepared for shipment by volunteers. The sheeting was sent to Istanbul in September with the help of Turkish airlines and was distributed by the local NGO, HSA

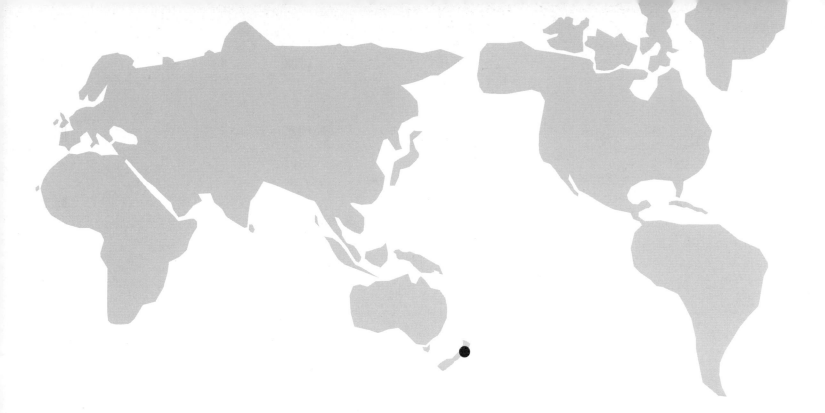

JASMAX Architects

THE NATIONAL TE PAPA TONGAREWA MUSEUM OF NEW ZEALAND

A bridge between cultures

Location **Wellington, New Zealand** Construction Period **1993-1998** Inauguration **1998** Client **The Board of The National Te Papa Tongarewa Museum of New Zealand** Structure, civil engineering, and construction **Holmes Arup Joint Venture** Geotechnics **Tonkin & Taylor** Seismic isolation **Skellerup Industries** Exhibition space consultants **Ralph Appelbaum & Associates** Photographs **JASMAX Architects**

Applicable seismic standard **NZS 4203**
Expected useful building life **150 years**
Number of earthquakes predicted during those 150 years: **5**

Expected period between earthquakes	Given intensities (Mercalli scale)	Likely damage	Probability
Every 250 years	**MM IX (maximum expected)**	**no significant damage**	**45%**
Every 500 years	**MM X**	**severe but repairable damage**	**26%**
Every 2,000 years	**MM XII (maximum imaginable)**	**should not collapse**	**7%**

Acceleration **Constant and substantially less than land acceleration**
Wind velocity **68 m/s**
The exhibition **Space includes an area devoted to earthquake simulation**

Total floor space of the building **395,000 sq. ft.**
The plan **Outdoor exhibition area (Harbour Park), Marae areas, usable by any New Zealander, for permanent exhibits, children's education center, traveling exhibition gallery, temporary exhibition area, storage areas, library, resource center, 350-seat auditorium, 50-seat theater, classrooms, restaurant and café, shop, workshop, offices, and 250-vehicle parking lot**
Total exhibition space **108,000 sq. ft.**

e Papa Tongarewa, the new national museum of New Zealand, an enormous, 395,000-square-foot building housing the country's cultural treasures, is spectacularly located on the waterfront in the center of the capital, Wellington, surrounded by mountains overlooking the bay. It replaced a small national museum which, from its very construction in 1936, was unable to house the whole collection. The new structure, designed to express all the nation's cultural nuances, dramatically altered the urban face of a city which has a rather limited urban profile because of its proximity to the mountains and sea, plus the earthquake risk. One of the quintessential characteristics of New Zealand is the way its two cultural influences, the European and the indigenous, coexist. This is reflected in the museum's fundamental aim: integrating the cultures and showing how they interact while bearing witness to and preserving their diversity.

This duality is reflected in the way the building has been situated on the bay and in its appearance and layout, a product of the complex set of objectives. The design was intended to serve as a transition between the orthogonal city and the openness of the sea, a bridge from the urban to the natural. Activities in the various areas of the building are linked according to their cultural origins. In addition to the permanent exhibits and the Marae, a traditional meeting space for Maoris, there is a children's education center, temporary exhibition galleries, shops, theaters, a library, a research center, offices, and a parking lot for 250 vehicles. The interaction with the landscape in the Harbour Park exposition area highlights the setting's natural features and allows the visitor to enjoy local flowers, fauna, and geology, culminating in an unusual, multiform geometric sculpture.

The building's structure and form are conditioned by local geographic and atmospheric characteristics. This area of the city and the entire waterfront are prone to flooding from the large waves produced by underwater tectonic movement. Wellington is also one of the most earthquake-prone regions of New Zealand, in addition to being susceptible to strong wind gusts. The basic building structure is a series of five-story-high concrete porticos reinforced by walls braced in only one direction, which means that most of the beams and slabs could be prefabricated. At the base of the structure is an economical, highly earthquake-resistant isolation system employing shock absorbing elements. Its principal advantage is the freedom it gaves to the rest of the structure (walls, external coverings, and flooring slabs) and the consequent design flexibility.

The city of Wellington forms a narrow line defined by the sea and mountains. The museum, given its complex design, was built on land reclaimed from the sea, forming a new peninsula

A model of the project prepared by JASMAX for the contest

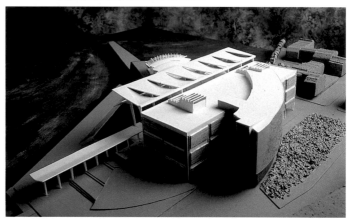

An aerial view of Wellington with the museum in the center

Partial view of Wellington's waterfront over the roof of Te Papa Tongarewa Museum's public entrance

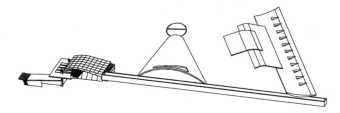

The roof

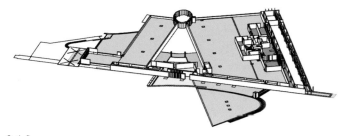

Sixth floor

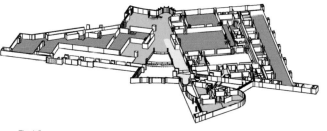

Fifth floor

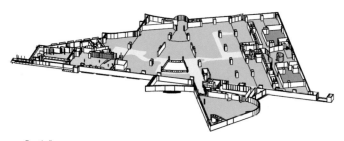

Fourth floor

Third floor

Second floor

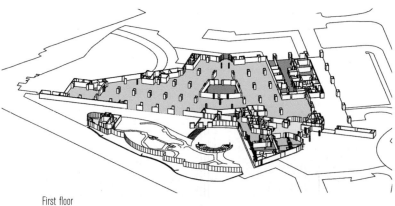

First floor

Exhibition gallery
Public access
Conference room
Shop
Administration, offices, and workshops
Service area and building systems
Collections
Parking lot

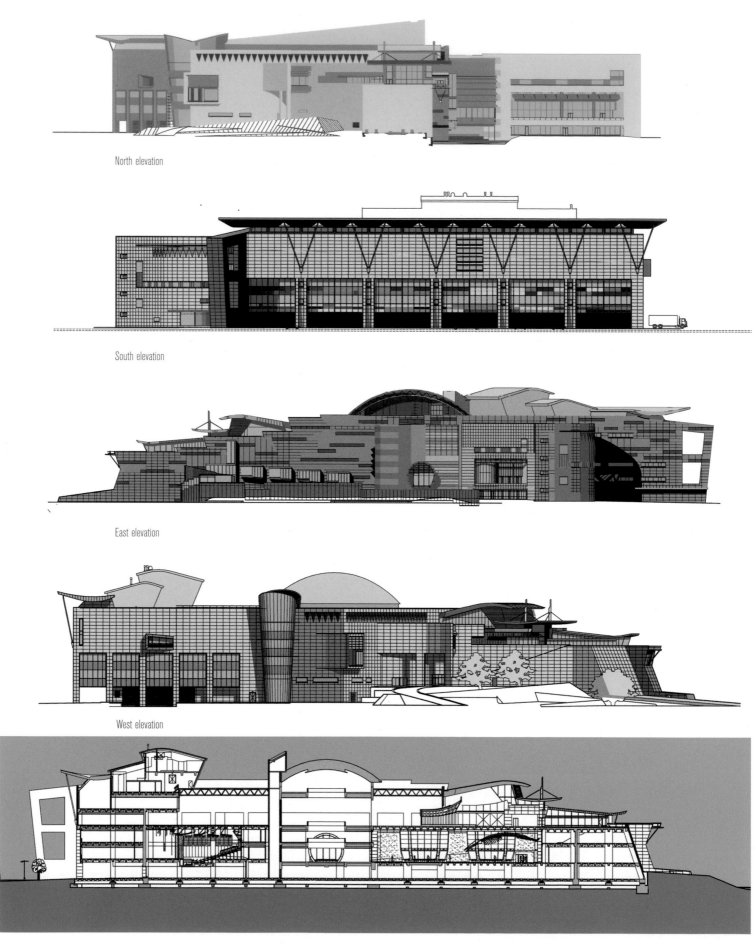

North elevation

South elevation

East elevation

West elevation

Cross-section

Above: View of the museum from Harbour Park

Below left: Exterior of the lobby

Below right: Close-up of the deck

Left: An interior view. A typical Marae door in the traditional style.

Right: Entrance to the Marae

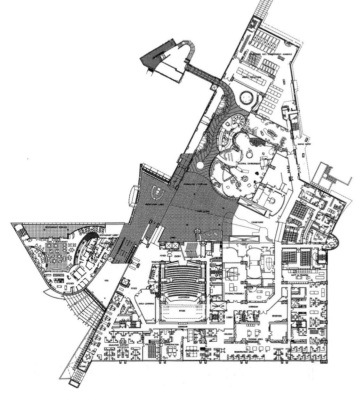

Second floor

Fourth floor

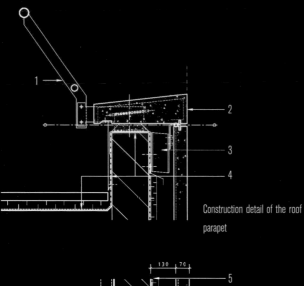

Construction detail of the roof parapet

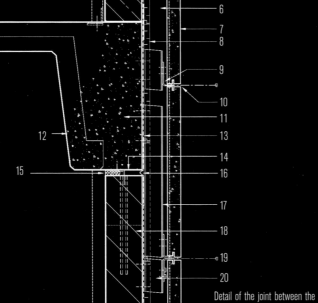

Detail of the joint between the framework and façade

1. Handrail
2. Prefabricated concrete fix
3. Support for gripping the covering
4. Closed horizontal and vertical joints
5. Closed joints
6. Air chamber
7. Prefabricated concrete panel
8. 50 mm. for isolation
9. Standard support and detail of the joint
10. 0,4 inches joint
11. Concrete in situ
12. Interior
13. Closed surfaces after isolation
14. Expansion joint
15. Fireproof material
16. Flexible, waterproof material to fill the 1 inch gap
17. Beam attached to the framework rather than the wall
18. Concrete block walls
19. Displacement joint
20. Support attached to the wall

I. Prefabricated concrete panel
2. Fireproof material
3. Aluminum window
4. Window frame
5. Window sill
6. Prefabricated material
7. Standard support and detail of joint
8. Prefabricated concrete panel

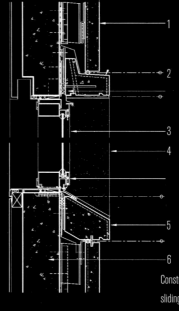

Construction detail of a standard sliding window

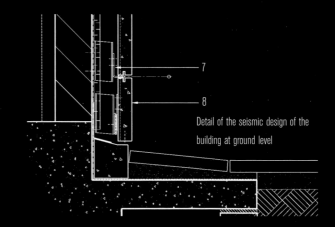

Detail of the seismic design of the building at ground level

The Te Papa Tongarewa Museum is protected from inclement weather by more than 15,000 prefabricated concrete exterior panels. Each piece, 6 ft. by 3 ft., and 1,80 inches thick, is held in place by stainless steel supports fastened to the inner concrete walls. This double skin counters the force of the rain and the winds

Left: Detail of the system which anchors the panels
Right: Partial view of the basalt panel-covering used on the façade

The isolating base, with 142 steel and rubber, lead-cored elements attached with screws, protects the building from seismic movements. Each isolator is placed between the foundation and the building structure, under the columns, to absorb part of the seismic energy transmitted through the ground. The effect of any tremors on the structure is mitigated since these pieces withstand horizontal earthquake oscillation, thus preventing structural collapse

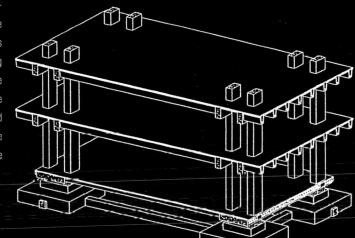

Diagram of the structural system

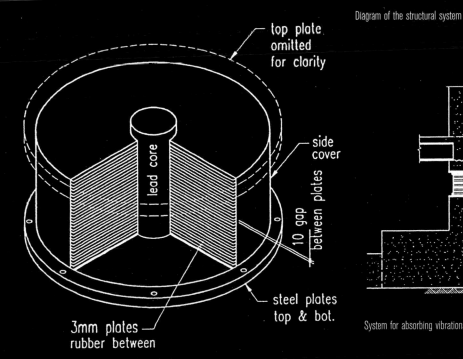

top plate omitted for clarity

side cover

lead core

10 gap between plates

steel plates top & bot.

3mm plates rubber between

Diagram of the support placed at the base of the pillars to absorb any seismic displacement

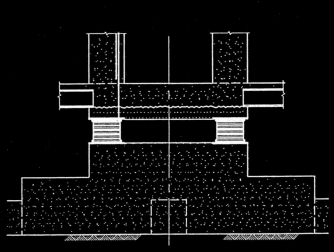

System for absorbing vibrations caused by potential earthquakes

Luis Izquierdo, Antonia Lehmann,
Raimundo Lira and José Domingo Peñafiel

MANANTIALES BUILDING

Spatial logotype of a real estate company

Location **Isidora Goyenechea, 3120. Santiago de Chile, Chile** Construction Dates **1998-1999** Client **Manantiales Construction Company** Construction company **SIGRO SA** Collaborator **Miguel Villegas** Design engineer **Luis Soler** Photographs **Guy St. Clair**

Applicable seismic code **Chilean seismic code Nch433 of 96**
Vibration period of the building **1.14 seconds**
Displacement at level 1 **Approx. 1.4"**
Permissible static tension in the ground **10 kg/cm²**
Permissible dynamic tension in the ground **12 kg/cm²**
Materials **H-35 reinforced concrete (resistance 350 kg/cm²), breaking under compression after 28 days; A63-42H steel**

Area of plot **19,430 sq. ft.**
Number of floors **17 above ground level and 5 underground**
Total floor space **102,150 sq. ft. above ground level and 75,420 sq. ft. underground**
Floor space of the two floor types **2583 sq. ft. and 7298 sq. ft.**
Use of the first floor **Shopping center**
Number of parking spaces **252**
Area per parking space **290 sq. ft.**

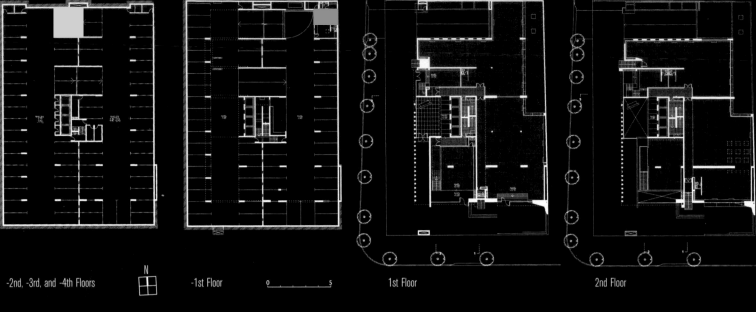

-2nd, -3rd, and -4th Floors

N

-1st Floor

0 _____ 5

1st Floor

2nd Floor

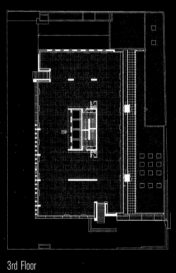

3rd Floor

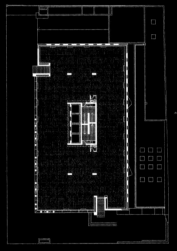

4th through 10th Floors

General view

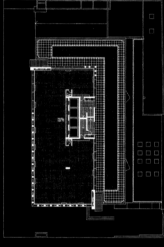

11th Floor

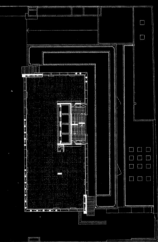

12th through 15th Floor

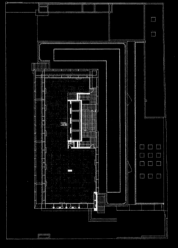

16th Floor

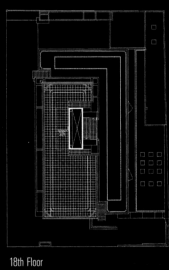

17th Floor

18th Floor

this office building is in a part of Santiago de Chile that has undergone significant changes in its urban form over the years. In the fifties–as part of a garden city plan– it contained detached houses. Later, due to the uncontrolled growth of the city all around this area and its great accessibility, it became one of the most exclusive neighborhoods in the city. The zone became more densely populated and the price per square foot is among the highest in Santiago. Although at first only residential buildings were constructed. However, as the years went by different activities began to appear on the scene. Now the area is defined by building of seven to twenty stories which are rarely in harmony with their immediate neighbors.

The mass and shape of the Manantiales Building are intended to blend in with its surroundings while making the most of the favorable urban conditions. The plot, on a corner in a landmark location, is actually five smaller plots combined. It is bordered by two buildings, ten and twelve stories high respectively. The architectural plan envisioned a seventeen-story building surrounded at the back by a ten-story L-shaped structure that fit in with the existing buildings. It is powerful in relation to its location, but comfortable vis-a-vis the irregular pattern of a neighborhood created in bits and pieces over the years.

Two fundamental factors influenced the design process. The financial necessities demanded that a high square foot price be charged. In response, the compact nuclear arrangement meant that whole floors could be put on the market as one unit, minimizing common, non-saleable areas. The other consideration was technical: the structure had to be flexible and resistant to ground movement. The project contains the offices of a property company and, at street level, retail stores. Shoppers and workers can park in one of the 252 underground spaces. The commercial attractiveness of the building is enhanced by the open plan design of the floors, which makes them adaptable to the demands of any type of office. The formal language of the façade reflects this flexibility–the floors, illuminated by the light flowing in, are visible from outside–.

The structural components were incorporated in a deliberate strategy to make the building exceptionally resistant. Consequently, the lowest part of the building, the service nucleus and the circulation areas, provide a rigid structure by means of walls. The columns, becoming smaller and less frequent as the building rises, ensure flexibility. The braces around the façade, especially on the topmost floors, allow any oscillations to be controlled. The exterior structure of unclad pillars and beams is visible from outside, providing a particularly expressive façade.

North elevation

East elevation

0 _____ 5

Reinforced non-traditional slabs were used so that large areas could be covered without a need for interior beams. This gave the floors tremendous flexibility and freedom from structural elements over vast areas. The ledges, inverted beams supported by cylindrical pillars, aided the placing of the office furniture and complied with fire regulations. Another plus is that they provide space for the air-conditioning vents and electrical wiring at the perimeter of the floors

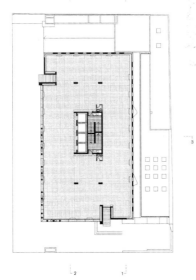

Standard office floor

0 — 5

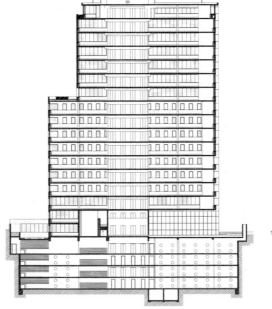

Interior of one of the office floors

The floors receive as much natural light as possible and enjoy views into the distance through sliding, high performance windows. Temperature is controlled without the need to add protection from the sun to the façade. The architectural interest is thereby focused on the structural solution and expression, which are exposed on the outside of the building

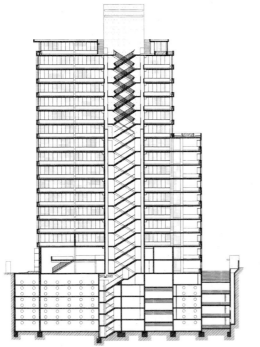

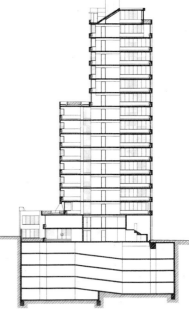

Longitudinal section 1-1

Longitudinal section 2-2

Cross section 3-3

Views of the entrance to the building

The structural asymmetry and rigidity produced by the perforated bearing walls are set in opposition to the elasticity of the pillars and beams forming the façade of the high-rise. Because the centers of gravity of the floors and the centers of rigidity are at a distance from each other, some turning and oscillation takes place on the higher stories. Rigidity-compensating reticular diagonals and pillars neutralize the problem

The structure was analyzed and designed seismically by bringing into play both rigid walls and inelastic frames to control horizontal forces and seismic lateral movements. Various dynamic tests were carried out to discover the optimum sections of the structure and to ensure that deformation values fell within the limits of Chilean seismic code Nch433 of 96. The figures obtained were a period of vibration for the building of 1.14 seconds and a displacement at level one of 3.5 centimeters

Close-up of the diagonal pillars

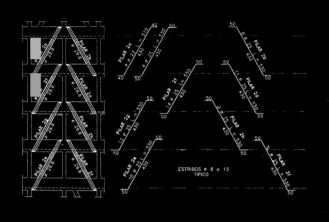

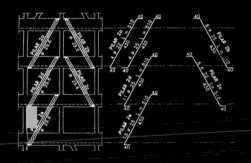

The pillars. Different aspects of the framework

0 _____ 5

The vertical pillars on the west face

Legorreta Arquitectos
METROPOLITAN CATHEDRAL OF MANAGUA
Reconstructing the city center

Location **Managua, Nicaragua** Construction date **1993** Client **Archdiocese of Managua** Promoter **Tom Monaghan (Domino's Pizza)** Structure **Walter P. Moore** Mechanical design **Lamsa Engineers**
Photographs **Lourdes Legorreta and Peter Cook**

Earthquakes history **Replaces the old Cathedral of Managua, destroyed by the 1972 earthquake that flattened the city center**

Site area **30 acres**

managua's new Metropolitan Cathedral, constructed in 1993, replaces the city's old cathedral, which was destroyed by the earthquake that flattened the center of the Nicaraguan capital in 1972. Restoration of the devastated area had to be postponed because of the economic crisis which beset the country in the 1970s. As a result, Managua began to acquire a unique urban configuration: while thick tropical vegetation took over in the all-but-ruined center, peripheral areas grew and the result was total disarray. Now, the capital has a rural look in some places because, especially in the historical center, the abundant vegetation almost causes existing buildings to disappear into the background. The Cathedral of Managua is designed not only to replace the old cathedral, but to become the city's new focus. Thus, this project–of enormous symbolic impact for Managuans–is an attempt to recover to some degree the civic center that for more than two decades was forced to wait in vain for rebirth, thereby offering the citizens a place of hope and unity.

The massive structure is located in the highest part of the city, on a 30-acre parcel. It is composed of a series of 63 domes which provide scale for the project and act as sources of light and ventilation.

The design embraces the new philosophy through which the contemporary Catholic community has moved from a passive role to a highly active, participatory one. The shorter distance between the people and priests, and the location of the highest dome in the central space and not (as is traditional) at one of the ends, exemplify the building's response to this concept. In addition, the cathedral broke with the typical process based on committee approval, permitting an emphasis on human and spiritual values in design and construction.

The project involves different scales, depending on the number of people who actually gather together to take part in the various church activities. Thus, on the two or three occasions each year when the cardinal celebrates mass for the nearly 100,000 people gathered at the entrance esplanade, he presides from the outside altar, over the main entrance. Inside, ceremonies periodically held in the central nave accommodate up to a thousand persons. In contrast, the Chapel of the Most Holy–whose scale and lighting convey intimacy–is the ideal setting for daily mass. Finally, the venerated image of the Blood of Christ is in a circular chapel which–through its shape, lighting, and colors–provides the icon an almost magical context.

Exposed concrete is used throughout. The floor, of handmade glazed tile, is designed in the form of a great carpet of geometrical figures. The doors and pews, large in proportion, are of light wood.

Despite the political conflicts that have plagued Nicaragua, the construction of the cathedral is evidence that–regardless of the differences and catastrophes–the community is able to join together for a single common aim: reconstruction of the city itself.

Rear façade, with chapel for daily mass on the left, sacristy in the center and the circular chapel dedicated to the image of the Blood of Christ on the right.
The Cathedral's entrance esplanade, where as many as 100,000 people may congregate on special occasions

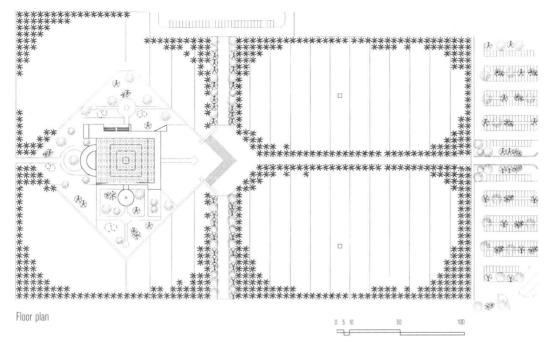

Floor plan

0 5 10   50   100

The Cathedral's floor.
Image of the Blood of Christ.
View of the central nave from the entrance.

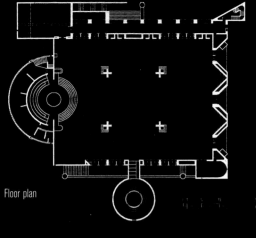

Floor plan

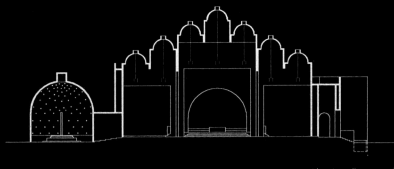

Transverse section.

63 domes open the central nave to natural light

Alberto Kalach

AUGEN ÓPTICOS LABORATORIES
A reference point on the landscape

Location **Ensenada, Baja California, Mexico** Construction period **1998-2000** Collaborator **Felipe Buendía** Client **Augen Ópticos** Structural engineer **Enrique Martínez Moreno** Builder **Absa Construcciones** Photos **Alberto Kalach**

Sesimic activity **Very high**
Seismic design **Scaly skin walls of 3/8 steel provide structural rigidity enabling it to withstand seismic forces and V-shaped columns absorb the vertical and horizontal forces of an earthquake**

Uses of the lower building **Offices and workshops**
Uses of the tower **Research**

ugen Ópticos, a firm dedicated to high-tech research and development in the field of lens making, commissioned architect Alberto Kalach to create two new buildings opposite the existing plant. When completed, the entire complex met the specific functional requirements of the laboratories perfectly and also addressed the danger of seismic activity. The work, fully capitalizing on the extraordinary sea views, has become a reference point on the landscape, a sculpted landmark for Ensenada in Baja California. The cylindrical tower, where research is conducted, is formed by walls of steel plate which, besides protecting the building from the sun's rays and taking the observer's eyes out over the sea, provide structural rigidity, enabling it to withstand seismic forces. The structural composition of the walls, which in a panoramic view seem like a scaly skin, allows the floors to be open. With a central mainstay providing tension, and support from the framework of the façade, the floors have neither pillars nor partitions: the space is flexible and unobstructed.

The low building, which houses offices and workshops, acts as a foundation for the entire complex. It is partially underground. A system of V-shaped columns, designed specifically for the project, provides a framework which supports the structure and allows it to remain lightweight. The columns absorb the vertical and horizontal forces produced by the occasional tremors which shake the area. The building has two very high-ceilinged stories with raised decks where complementary program activities take place.

Above: Research tower.
Below: Offices and workshops building

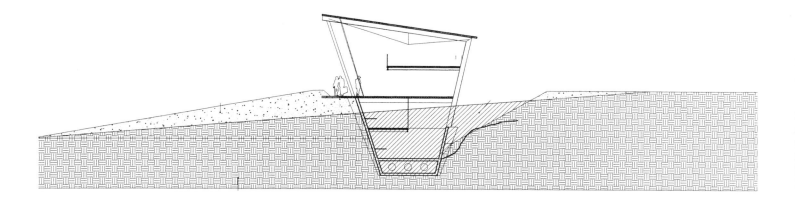

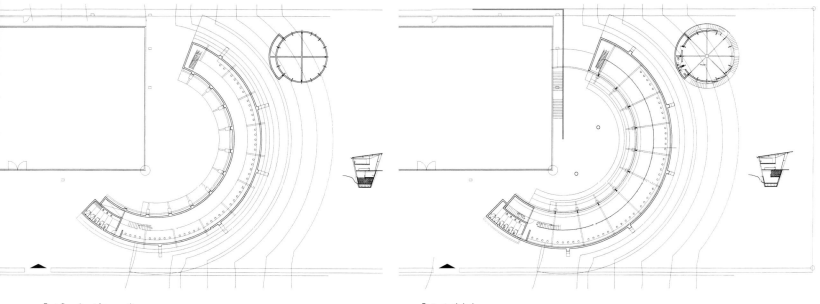

First floor (semi-basement)

First raised deck

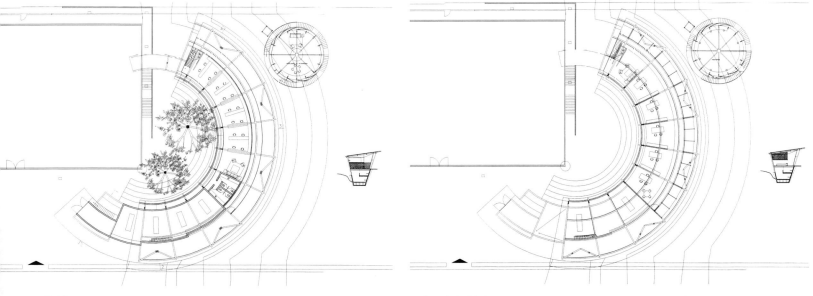

First floor

Second raised deck

Building floors and workshops.

North general view

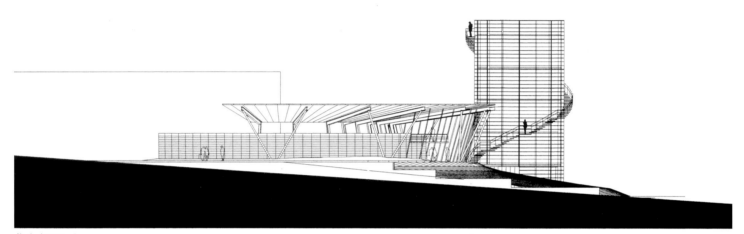

North elevation

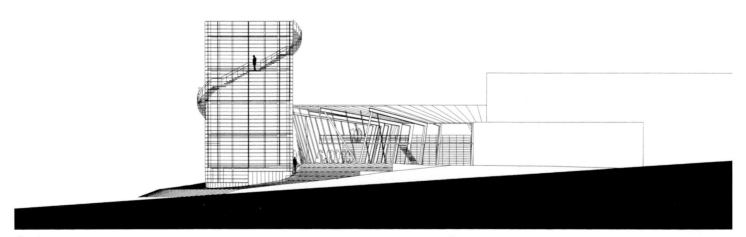

East elevation

Close-up of the staircase, almost a sculptural element at the building's base

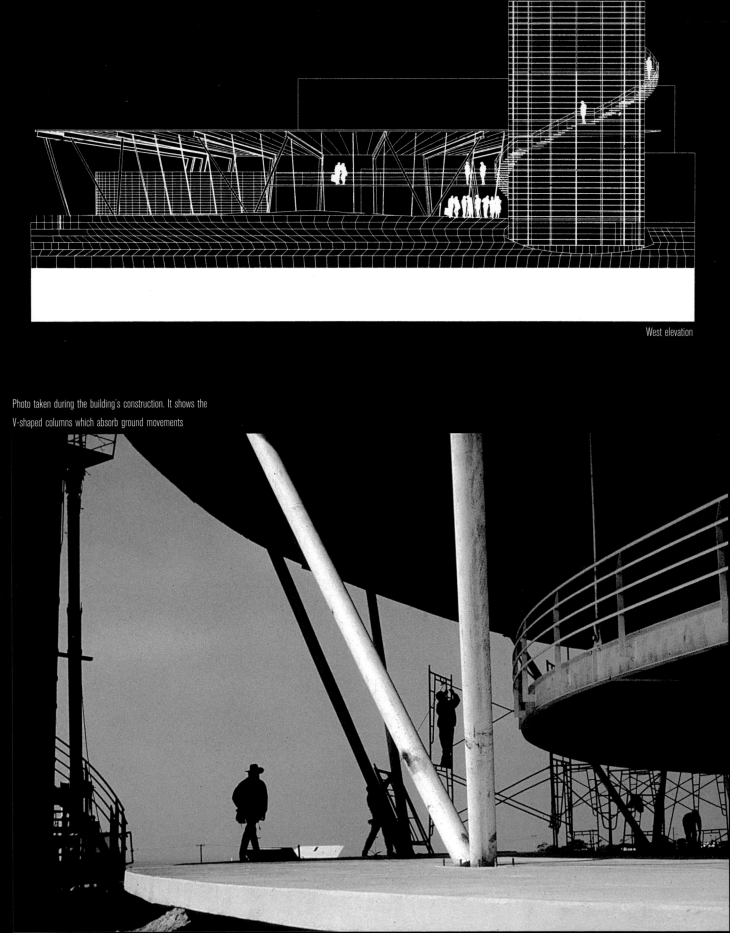

West elevation

Photo taken during the building's construction. It shows the
V-shaped columns which absorb ground movements

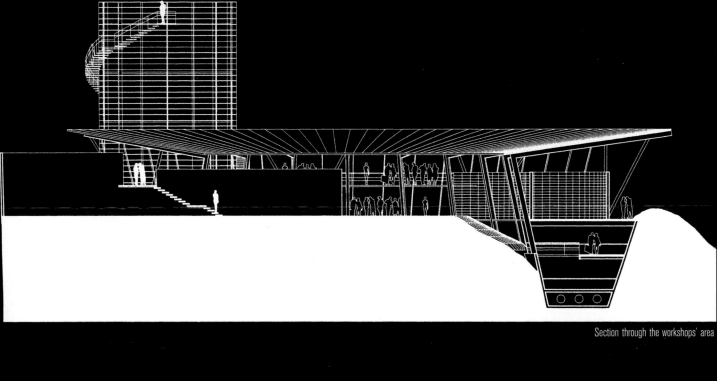

Section through the workshops' area

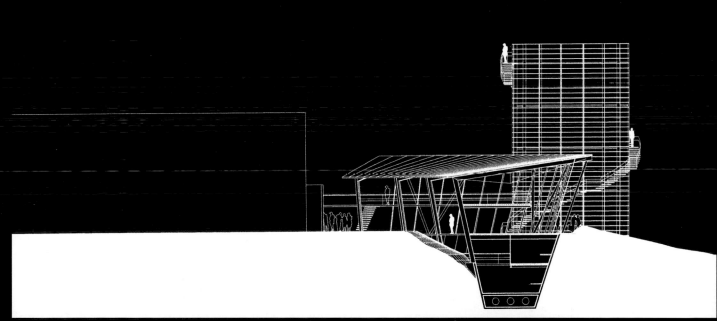

Section through the administration area

Details of the roof's support (left and center) and view from the interior of the scaly skin on the façade (right)

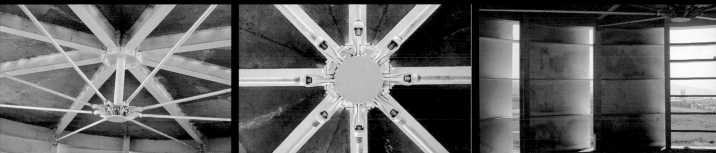

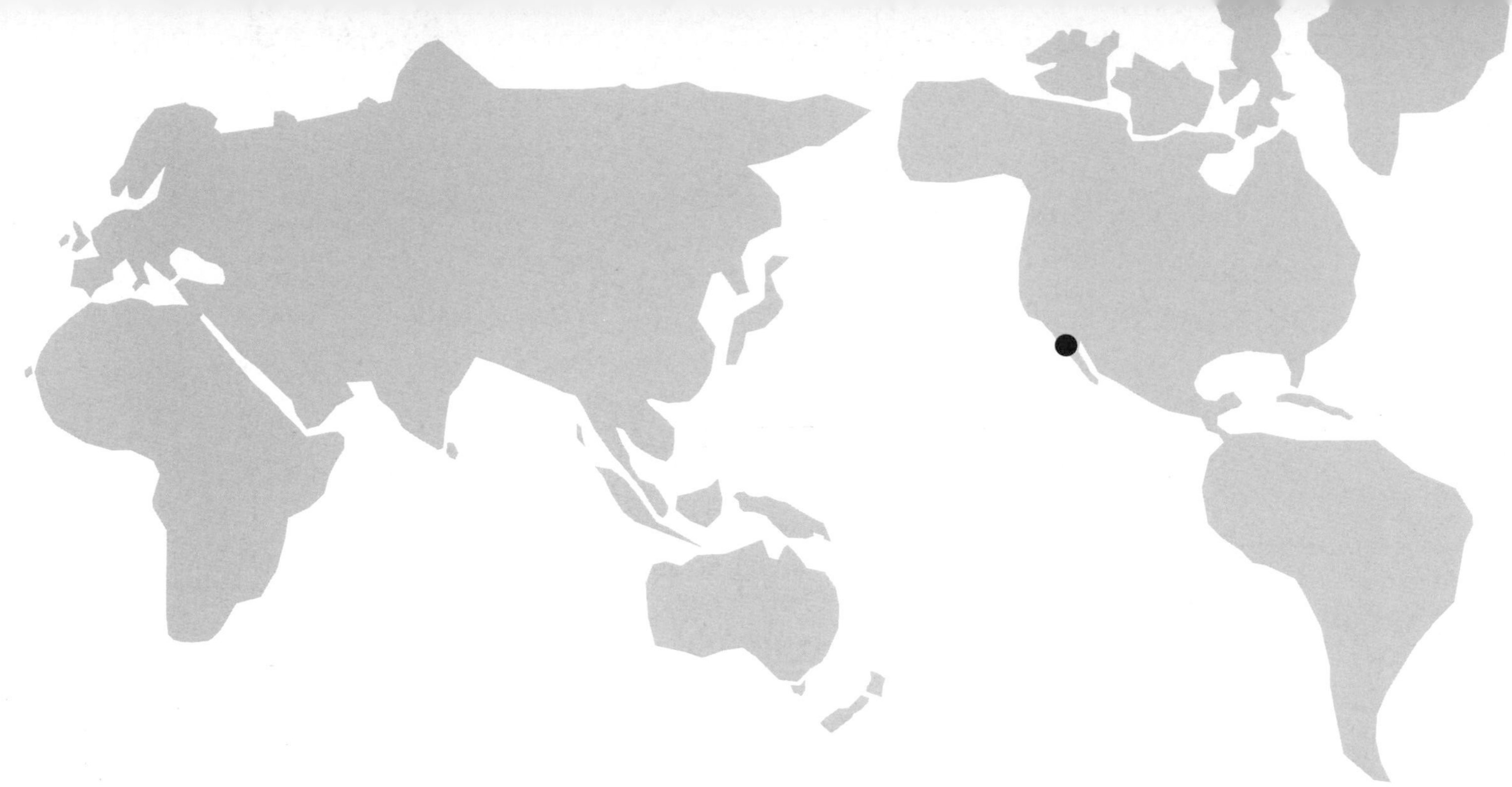

BTA-Bobrow/Thomas & Associates

ARROWHEAD REGIONAL MEDICAL CENTER

A hospital complex to maintain

Associated architects **Perkins & Will (Chicago)** Location **Colton, California, U.S.A.** Construction date **1999** Client **San Bernardino County** Construction company **JCM Group (Los Angeles)** Engineers **KPFF Consulting Engineers in association with Taylor & Gaines (Pasadena)** Contractors **McCarthy/Obayashi (Newport Beach)** Photography **John Linden** Last published photographs **Appeared in "Engineering News Record", September 11, 1995;** ^c**The McGraw-Hill Companies Inc. All rights reserved**

Earthquake history **"Northridge", January 1994, during the final design process**

Seismic resistance **Magnitude 8.5 on the Richter scale**

Designation **Since its construction, considered to have the greatest seismic resistance of any public building in the world**

Resources **In case of earthquake, it can remain self-sufficient for at least three days**

Seismic risk **Very high, since it is located approximately 2 miles from the San Jacinto Fault and 9 miles from the San Andreas Fault**

Number of base isolators **392**

Total cost of portals **$7,000,000**

Total cost of seismic isolation system **$10,000,000**

Percentage of total cost dedicated to seismic design **10%**

Gross building area **920,000 sq. ft.**

Site area **3,930,000 sq. ft.**

Number of beds **873**

Total cost **$276,000,000**

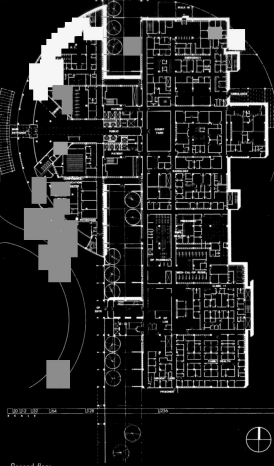

Second floor

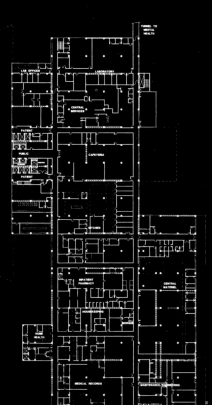

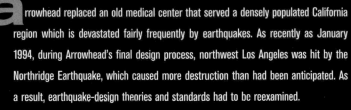

rrowhead replaced an old medical center that served a densely populated California region which is devastated fairly frequently by earthquakes. As recently as January 1994, during Arrowhead's final design process, northwest Los Angeles was hit by the Northridge Earthquake, which caused more destruction than had been anticipated. As a result, earthquake-design theories and standards had to be reexamined.

BTA won the construction bid for the medical center in 1990 with a state-of-the-art, functional project conceived from the inside out, sufficiently flexible to incorporate future developments.

A complex inside a park, the center's functions are distributed among five buildings linked by a north-south pedestrian promenade. This placement helps delineate and separate the medical facilities from buildings housing other services. It also provides each module with autonomous exterior space as well as optimum lighting and ventilation. The tallest structure, a half-cylinder with a panoramic view of the valley, contains hospital rooms. Other services are in orthogonal structures with interior patios connected by exterior promenades with small plazas where people can rest. None of the buildings blocks the mountain view from downtown.

The separation offers other advantages: clearly established interior organization and layout, easy differentiation of the various hospital facilities, structural detachment of each blocks in relation to the complex—favoring suitable performance in an earthquake—and, finally, easy evacuation in case of emergency.

Although functionally connected, the different buildings are structurally independent. Three are joined by innovative 14-foot-long corridors, called portals. During earthquakes, these allow the space separating the buildings to contract by four inches or expand by as much as eight feet.

The medical center's foundation has a passive hybrid damping system comprised of 392 rubber supports and a series of shock absorbers. Under each metal column is a damping device that allows the entire structure to maintain its original position, with the system absorbing any earth movement.

Given the high seismic risk of the site—barely 9 miles from the San Andreas and San Jacinto faults—the complex was designed to withstand earthquakes up to a magnitude of 8.5 on the Richter scale. It is also self-sufficient and can be fully operational without recourse to outside supplies for 72 hours. These uncompromising strategies have made the medical center the most earthquake resistant public building in existence.

off-site, the building containing the hospital rooms
with the ground floor entrance and, finally, partial
view of the south façade with the north-south
promenade at lower left

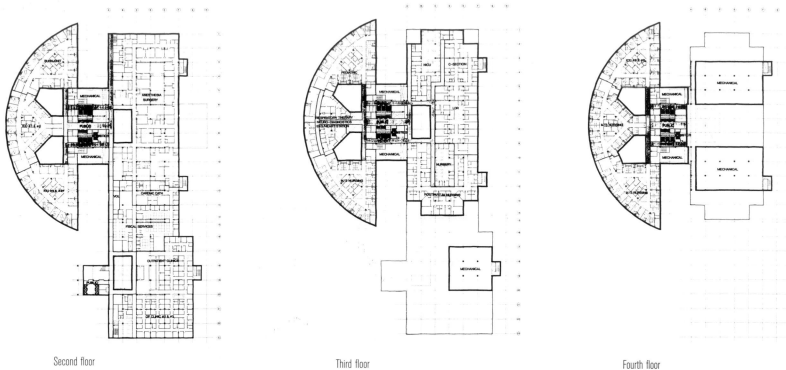

Second floor

Third floor

Fourth floor

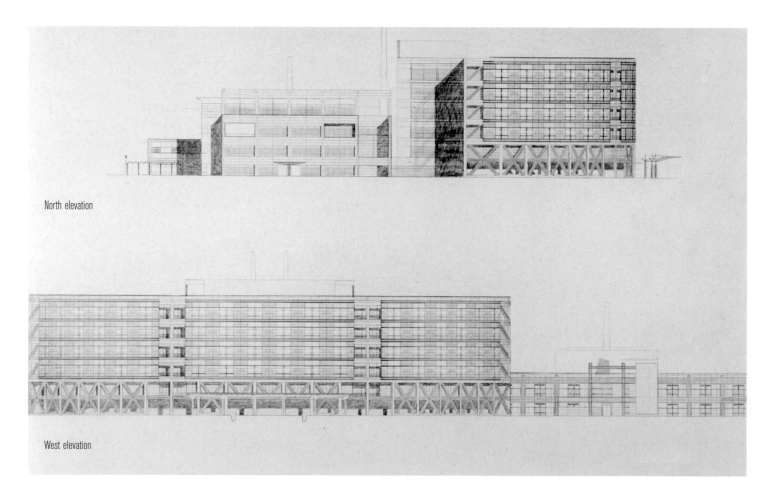

North elevation

West elevation

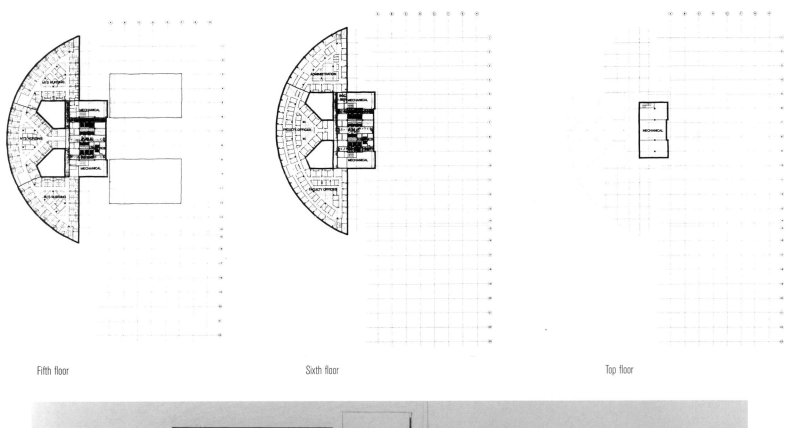

Fifth floor

Sixth floor

Top floor

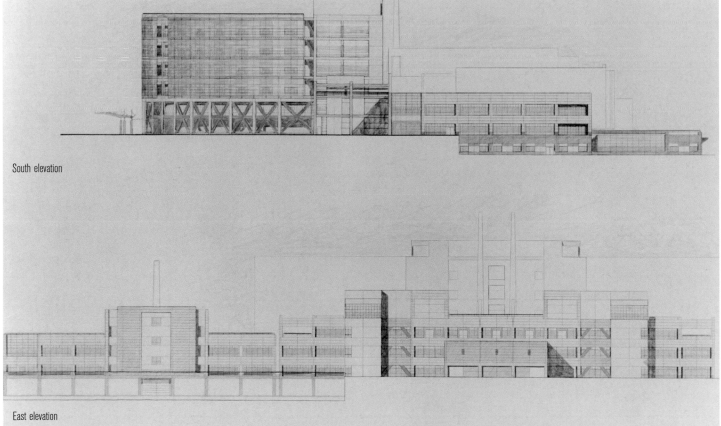

South elevation

East elevation

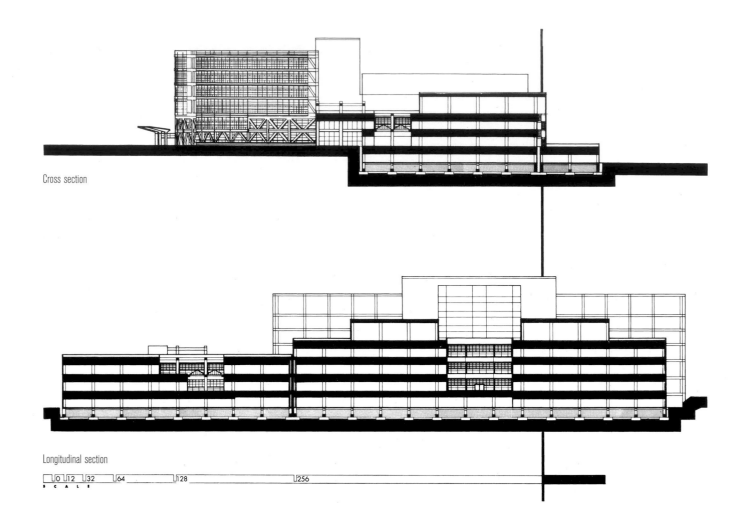

Cross section

Longitudinal section

SCALE: 0 12 32 64 128 256

Light and optimum ventilation play fundamental roles inside.
Most of the materials are white or light gray, lessening the
differences perceived among the various components

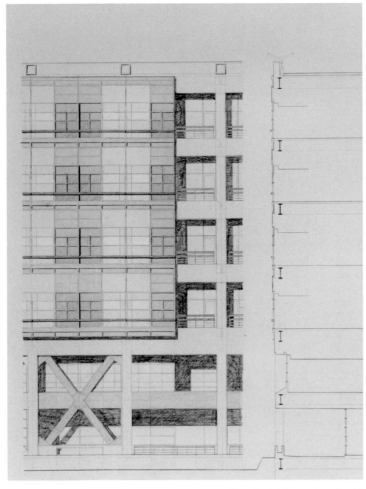

Above: Detail of the elevation and partial view of the metal structure of the semi-cylindrical building.
Left: The bracing on the first floor will considerably improve the structure's behavior in the event of earthquake

While the isolators reduce the structure's displacement, the damping devices control ground acceleration. The isolators, approximately 20 inches high and 35 inches in diameter, with rubber disks sandwiched between steel plates, are placed under columns and walls to carry vertical loads.

The damping devices, about 12 feet long and 12 inches in diameter, closely resemble automobile shock absorbers. Maintenance-free, stainless steel pistons inside silicon-filled cylinders, specially manufactured for Arrowhead Medical Center, are installed horizontally with one end joined to the foundation and the other joined to the end of a column or beam. Capable of absorbing the energy from an earthquake, they were adapted from the system designed to protect MX missiles from a nuclear explosion

Passive hybrid damping system

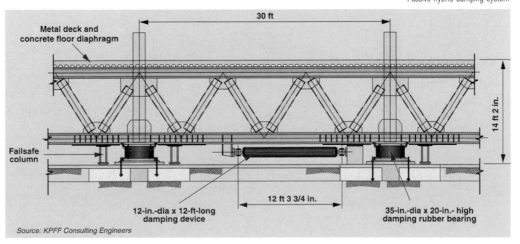

Metal deck and concrete floor diaphragm

30 ft

14 ft 2 in.

Failsafe column

12-in.-dia x 12-ft-long damping device

12 ft 3 3/4 in.

35-in.-dia x 20-in.- high damping rubber bearing

Source: KPFF Consulting Engineers

Eugene Tsui (Tsui Design and Research Inc.)

RESIDENCE FOR FLORENCE AND WILLIAM TSUI

Nature as the origin of architecture

Location **Berkeley, California, U.S.A.** Construction period **1993-1995** Clients **Florence and William Tsui**

Earthquake-resistant design A system of recycled styrofoam/cement blocks reinforced with steel and concrete. The material is extremely resistant to ground shaking and is also light, fire-resistant, waterproof, and termite-proof

Structurally, the unit has a reinforced network that distributes stresses uniformly. The continuous ellipse of the walls forms an extremely resistant frame and was chosen because of its rigid lateral properties

Surface area **3,500 sq. ft.**
Arrangement **Four bedrooms, three bathrooms, dining room, living room, patio-garden and garage**
Cost **$270,000**

In a quiet residential neighborhood of Berkeley, California, Florence and William Tsui's strangely shaped house emerges, forcefully interrupting the monotonous pattern of stereotypical one-family American suburban homes. The owners wanted a house that would protect their privacy and that was free of stairs, with spaces opening onto each other where they could exhibit artwork. It also had to be well-lighted and earthquake-proof, with central heating and air-conditioning, and have absolutely waterproof foundations.

The project's creator, the architect and designer Eugene Tsui, offered them an ellipse. This geometry answered the clients' initial needs and provided a programmatic image of their elaborate conception. Tsui has written a theoretical work, *Evolutionary Architecture* (1999), outlining his entire creative vision, which is based on the infinite possibilities of nature as the foundation of architectural design.

Outside, the house's concave walls curve in at a 4-degree angle to form a unitary structure with a low center of gravity which will also strengthen resistance to stresses and strains from the strong tremors in the area. Tsui believes this structure is preferable to traditional, old-fashioned orthogonal shapes, which he strongly opposes as examples of a stale rationalism that is unable to meet the biological, physical, and emotional needs of the human dwelling.

The continuity of the elliptic form distributes loads uniformly and tangentially to the surface, thereby avoiding concrete load centers that could damage the entire building. Since the walls, are curved, they deflect and accelerate the wind currents playing on the surface and prevent the vacuum effect planes are subject to and related high fire risk. In addition, a ring of four water jets increases the exterior wall's protection from any fire in the vicinity.

The entire building design alludes to living organisms and their ability to actively confront the area's various natural forces. The solar air tubes provide one notable example. Located on the south wall to take advantage of the sunlight, they cover much of the upper part of the house. The air in the black tubes is heated by the sun during the day, and at night the stored heat is returned to the walls, radiating heat inward. This heating system was inspired by study of the bones and capillary structures of two dinosaur species whose thermal systems consisted of a bony structure surrounded by a compact configuration of blood vessels that stored heat from the outside during the day.

Nature's evolutionary course is present throughout the building, a complex, emerging form which, through its deceptively futuristic shape, assumes no more than an approximation of the origin, the archetypal moment at which Tsui finds all the answers to the enigmas architecture presents.

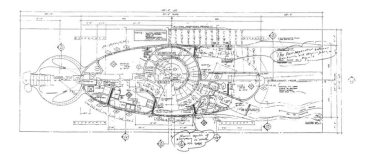

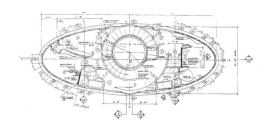

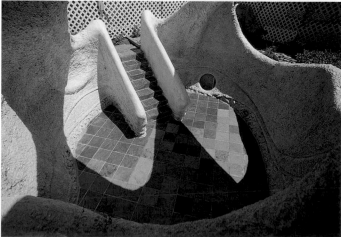

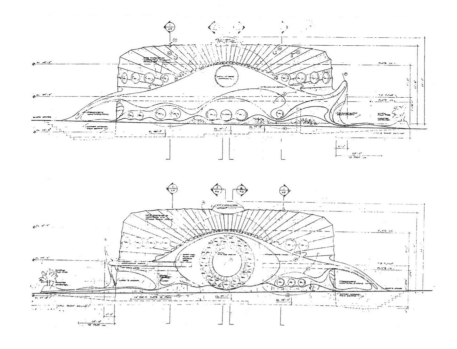

Tsui believes this structure is preferable to traditional,
old-fashioned orthogonal shapes

View of the interior and detail of one window

As requested by the owners, there are no stairs inside the Tsui house. The architects designed a complex set of multiple levels connected by a series of spiral ramps, culminating in a final circular ramp in the center of the house. The name of the building, Tai Yang Yen—Sun's Eye—comes from the south-facing 14-foot round window (oculus), which allows sunlight to warm the interior floors. Heat which accumulates during the day is thus distributed later, when it is needed. The use of multiple resources to optimize solar energy efficiency is perhaps the design leitmotiv of the structure

Pulverized cement is applied to tubes and joints. While the concrete is still wet, a special brush is used to make grooves on the surface to improve its resistance to wind and fire

Architect's drawing

Parabolic structure. The 4-degree inward slant of the walls creates a stable center of gravity for the building. The wood layers are spread on a frame, creating a tight, rigid surface

Images of the construction process

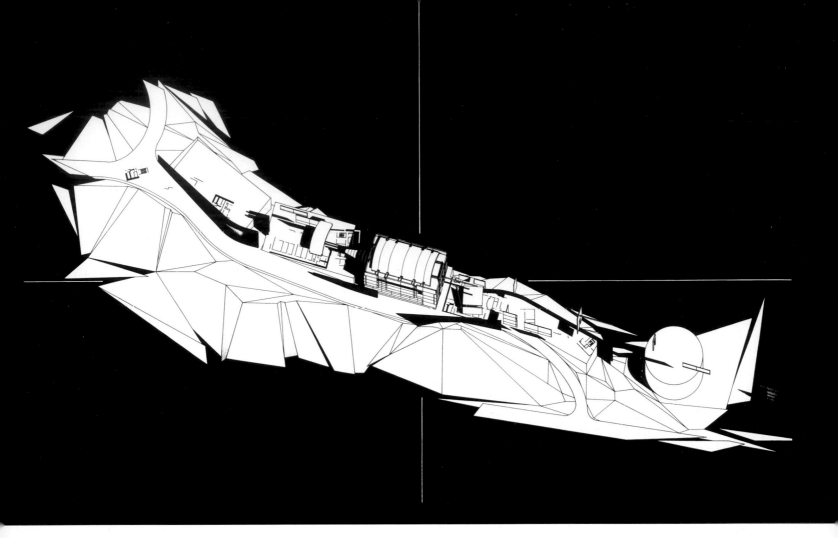

BTA-Bobrow/Thomas & Associates

LOS ANGELES EMERGENCY OPERATIONS CENTER

A smart building

Associated Architects **Daniel, Mann, Johnson & Mendelhall (DNJM)** Location **Los Angeles, California, U.S.A.** Construction date **1995** Client **City of Los Angeles**

Relationship to earthquakes In the event of any disaster, natural or otherwise, the operations center carries out centralized data processing to coordinate emergency work in the area Resistance to earthquakes Magnitude 8.3 on the Richter scale

Gross building area 28,000 sq. ft.
Total cost $9,000,000

In recent years, disasters of widely differing origin have affected southern California. Social unrest, fires, earthquakes, and floods, among other things, have demonstrated the need for a single point from which the tasks of the various emergency operation teams could be centralized and coordinated in critical situations. In response, the City of Los Angeles proposed the creation of an operations center to deal with future emergencies.

The center occupies the crest of a hill facing eastern Los Angeles, totally dominating the surrounding areas both visually and electronically. Its design, clearly reflecting the building's purpose, aims at establishing an extremely efficient and secure point of control to facilitate decision making in times of crisis.

The operations center is integrated into the landscape by means of low concrete walls. The main structure, of prefabricated concrete with a warm gray finish, is crowned by a stucco-finished barrel roof. Three shafts provide constant ventilation for the interior, while openings in the upper part allow light to enter. The building appears self-contained, set off from its environs. In contrast, the large communications tower draws in and engages the surrounding area.

In an emergency, the operations center can be self-sufficient for at least a week. In addition, in an earthquake, the structure's isolation from the terrain allows it to withstand tremors of up to magnitude 8.3 on the Richter scale.

The main building is connected by a pedestrian bridge to a terraced parking platform. The small vaulted roof which frames and protects the main entrance echoes the shape of the building's roof.

Inside, beyond the main entrance, a large reception area ensures total control of building access. Floor-to-floor circulation and service areas are located on the perimeter, constituting a kind of band enclosing the main area, a double-height room where data processing and decision making are carried out, and around which the space is organized. A continuous corridor circles the building, connecting the offices. In addition, translucent panels divide these offices, allowing natural light to reach the interior of the operations center. An outside balcony on the north side of the building permits observation of the surrounding countryside.

The delicate nature of the emergency operations center's purpose is reflected in the simple way in which the designers have tried to work out both the interior and the exterior layout of the complex. The building must, above all, be easy to use when needed in any kind of disaster.

Whole plan.

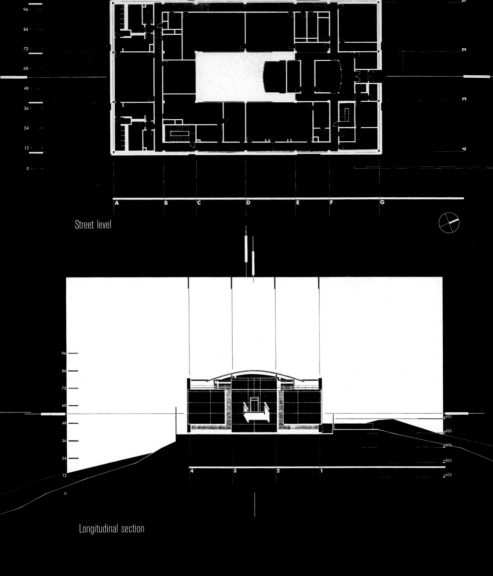

Street level

Longitudinal section

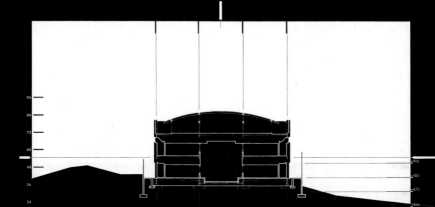

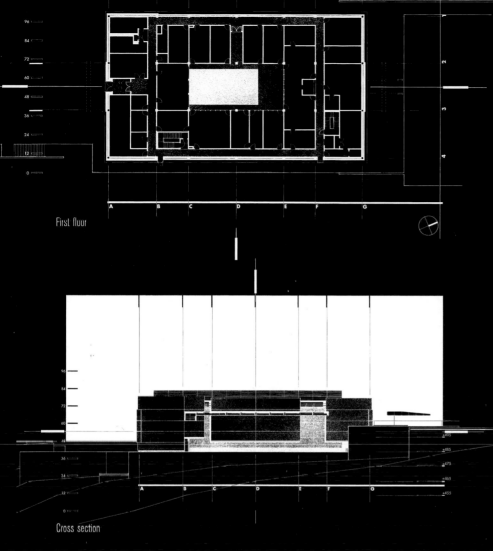

First floor

Cross section

Pei Cobb Freed & Partners
FIRST INTERSTATE WORLD CENTER
Los Angeles Landmark

Location **Los Angeles, California, U.S.A.** Construction date **1987-1989** Client **Maguire Thomas Partners (Santa Monica), in association with Pacific Enterprises (Los Angeles)** Structure **CBM Engineers, Inc.** Geotechnics **Leroy Crandall & Associates** Photographs **Jane Lidz, Hedrich Blessing, Warren Aerial Photography (Los Angeles); ©Aker/Zvonkovic Photography (Houston)** Map Appeared in "Engineering News Record", September 14, 1989; ©The McGraw Hill Companies Inc. All rights reserved Plans **Pei Cobb Freed & Partners** Final image **CBM Engineers**

Seismic resistance **Magnitude 8.3 on the Richter scale (maximum required for this zone)**
Seismic risk **Very high because of its location on terrain with several faults, some 40 miles from the San Andreas Fault**
Seismic predictions **A large earthquake, the much feared "Big One," is expected in this zone**

Total exterior height **1,034 ft.**
Number of stories **73 above ground level (plus two floors for system installations and helipad) and 2 below ground level (parking)**
Site area **1.4 acre**
Total area of the building **1,751,840 sq. ft.**
Total commercial area **44,455 sq. ft.**
Total office area **1,340,656 sq. ft.**
Total parking area **200,210 sq. ft.**
Typical Floor, First Tier **23,035 sq. ft.**
Typical Floor, Second Tier **19,050 sq. ft.**
Typical Floor, Third Tier **17,010 sq. ft.**
Typical Floor, Fourth Tier **12,490 sq. ft.**
Typical Floor, Fifth Tier **9,040 sq. ft.**
Parking capacity **547 cars**

General aerial view

the decision to erect this enormous tower, the highest on the West Coast of the U.S.A., was influenced by specific factors relevant to this part of Los Angeles. Vertical architecture has never suited this city because of the many faults that lie beneath its streets. But the commitment to preserve some of the area's historic buildings and the desire to have a landmark in the city center formed the rationale for this project. The site is directly between the established city center and the Bunker Hill area, on a slight rise, in a locale undergoing multiple-use urban development. The City of Los Angeles wanted to strengthen the link between the two areas, consolidating the city's civic center through a commercial and office-building complex, while avoiding the proposed demolition of one of the city's few architectural gems, the Los Angeles Central Library. The team of architects therefore planned a 73-story building, right across the street from the library, which would incorporate all of the elements of the complicated plan for the area. This would also accomplish another municipal objective: building an obelisk-like point of reference in the city center. The project, as backdrop for the library and the staircase that connects it with Bunker Hill, is seen at street level not as an object but rather as one more actor on the urban stage, where the unchallenged protagonist is the Los Angeles Central Library.

The idea of having a structure that would link these two areas of Los Angeles like a joint, as well as the significant construction demands, were the two main determinants of the building's configuration. The resulting squared cylinder organizes and gives form to the building while meeting the established requirements. The square permits optimal use of interior space, and the circle speaks to the urban plane and to the neighborhood itself. The radial and orthogonal forms are also seen in the observatory windows, which emphasize the tower's height, provide fantastic panoramas of the city, and reduce the perception of the building as a solid mass. The building has light granite walls that frame the volumes created by the windows and animate the façade as the sun's rays play on it throughout the day.

Local earthquake risk conditions defined the building's structural system and, thus, its resulting composition. The project, some 1034 feet high, was designed to withstand an earthquake of up to 8.3 on the Richter scale. A framework capable of managing the conflicting demands of earthquake (flexibility) and wind (rigidity) was needed, using simple structural elements. The system includes a resistant steel frame on the outside perimeter of the tower, designed as the ductile element to absorb seismic movement, with a squared rigid internal body, extending the entire height of the building.

These geometric and structural elements combine to create a rich visual perspective and a very specific architectural identity, while making the First Interstate World Center a reference point from both the neighborhood streets and from great distances. It has now become a part of the L.A. skyline.

The great height, the panels forming the lobby entrance which soften the lines of the space, and the combination of natural and artificial light give the entrance both an interior and exterior feel

Analysis of building reaction to one
of the 32 vibration types studied

The combination of the two structural
systems, the rigid internal core and the
flexible perimeter, provides the building
with sufficient lateral strength to withstand
both high-velocity winds and strong
ground motion. The base of the core is
reinforced with two-story-high chevroned
braces. This system, which is used here
for the first time in a large-scale building,
makes possible the tower's large window
openings and its apparent lack of
structural elements

Typical floors

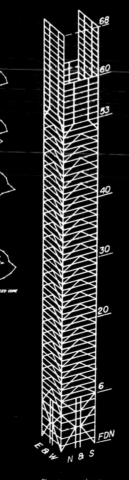

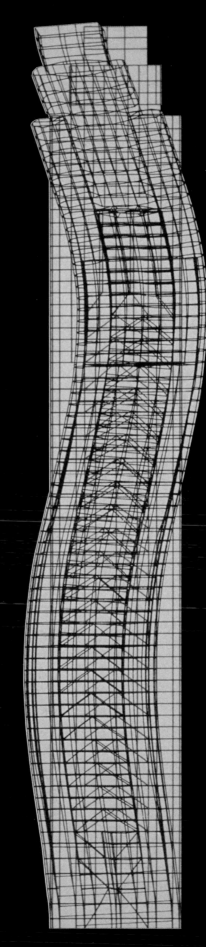

Axonometric drawing of the perimeter

Elevator core bracing

SOM (Skidmore, Owings & Merrill LLP)

EXPANSION AND RENOVATION OF THE SAN FRANCISCO COURT OF APPEALS

A historic building strengthened

Associated architects **Perkins & Will (Chicago)** Location **San Francisco, California, U.S.A.** Construction period **1993-1997** Clients **General Services Administration, Pacific Region-Administrative Office of the Ninth District Court** Collaborators **Craig Hartman (design); Ed McCrary, Fred Powell (project leaders); Sharon Cox, Steve Weindel (representatives of the firm)** Structural engineering **Navin Amin, Hamid Fatehi, Peter Lee, Anoop Mokha** Construction company **Clark Construction** Lighting **Flack + Kurtz Consulting Engineers Claud Engel** Historical architect **Page & Turnbull** Interior decorating **Tamara Dinsmore** Photography **Abby Sadin**

Earthquake history **The 1906 earthquake and the Loma Prieta earthquake (1989)**
Seismic resistance **Magnitude 8.0 on the Richter scale**
Seismic design **256 base isolators located in the original structure allow the building to sway**

Gross building area **366,000 sq. ft.**
Cost **$91,000,000**

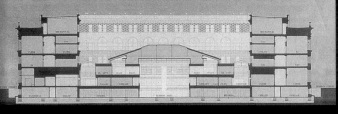

East-west longitudinal section of the library

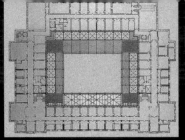

Second floor

Third floor

Exterior view of the Court of Appeals

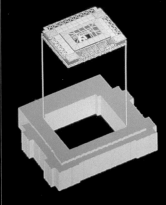

The glass-and-metal structure covering the
atrium of the law library reading room

Detail of the new skylight, which
reconfigured the existing space

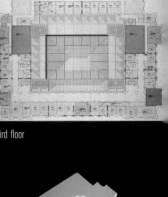

t he San Francisco Court of Appeals renovation and expansion project met the challenges of two different and equally demanding goals. First, the almost 100-year-old building needed appropriate technological and structural improvements to prevent earthquake damage. Second, it also needed to blend the old with the new, while dealing with the inherent risks of any highly literal renovation. In this case, it appears that both goals were optimally satisfied.

The San Francisco Court of Appeals, a historic, Beaux Arts building designed by James Knox Taylor in 1905, survived two of the most devastating earthquakes the city of San Francisco has known in the last 100 years: the famous 1906 earthquake, magnitude 8.3 on the Richter scale, and the 1989 earthquake, magnitude 7.1. The more recent quake, known as the Loma Prieta, seriously damaged the building, which had to be closed for repair and renovation.

The team in charge of the upgrade, Skidmore, Owings and Merrill (SOM), faced with the forbidding presence of a building of such imposing size and mass, engaged in a two-pronged earthquake resistance strategy: finding the appropriate isolators and determining where they should be placed. After several attempts by the Earthquake Engineering Research Center of the University of California at Berkeley, the solution was found: a friction pendulum system (FPS) would be placed above the foundation and below the basement. Each of the main columns was cut, then supported on hydraulic jacks. A total of 256 pendulum bearings, concave stainless steel cylinders, were attached under the top part of the severed columns, which were repositioned on sliders attached to the top of the lower section of the columns. As a result, the whole building, resting on these new supports, can rock as a single unit in the event of earthquake pressure. Thanks to the concave disks, the building can even rise slightly, sliding some two feet on the steel bowl. Testing by the University of Berkeley concluded that the structure would withstand an earthquake of magnitude 8.0 on the Richter scale.

The friction pendulum system, used for the first time in a historic building, also resulted in a gain of nearly 40,000 sq. ft. of floor space in the courthouse basement.

Since the Court of Appeals is protected by the National Register of Historic Places, it was necessary to maintain the original structure and clearly delineate the various new elements from those belonging to the previous architecture.

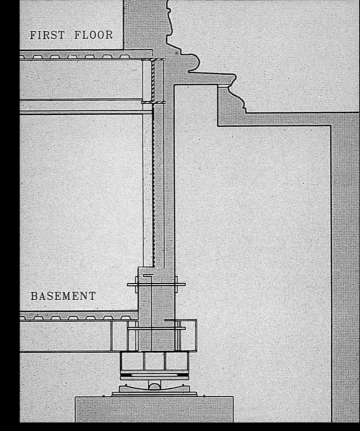

FIRST FLOOR

BASEMENT

Detail of a friction pendulum bearing

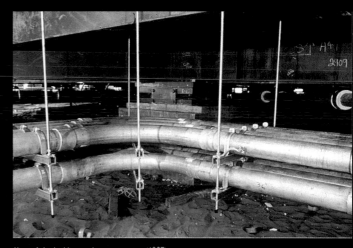

View of the building under construction (1997)

Detail of the sliding disks in a friction pendulum bearing

SOM (Skidmore, Owings & Merrill LLP), Del Campo & Maru and Michael Willis Associates

NEW INTERNATIONAL TERMINAL FOR SAN FRANCISCO AIRPORT

The sensation of lightness

Location **San Francisco, California, U.S.A.** Construction period **1993-2000** Client **San Francisco Airport Commission** Plan director **Daniel, Mann, Johnson & Mendelhall - 1989** Bid **1993** Building company Engineers **Skidmore, Owings & Merrill LLP** Photographs **Hedrich Blessing, Abby Sadin and SOM**

Earthquake history during the design process **"Northridge", January 17, 1994, magnitude 6.7 on the Richter scale**
Status of the terminal on January 17, 1994 **In the planning stages**
Effects of the earthquake **The architects became aware of the need to strengthen the seismic design criteria**
Recurrence period **1,000 years**
Seismic criteria **The seismic measures are the most exacting ever applied in the United States**

Number of floors **5**
Total surface area **6.4 sq. m.**
Surface area devoted to restaurants and businesses **140,000 sq. ft.**
Total cost of modernization and expansion program **$500,000,000**
Total cost **$993,000,000**

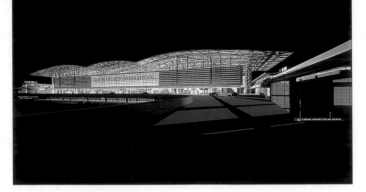

General view of the planned expansion of the international terminal

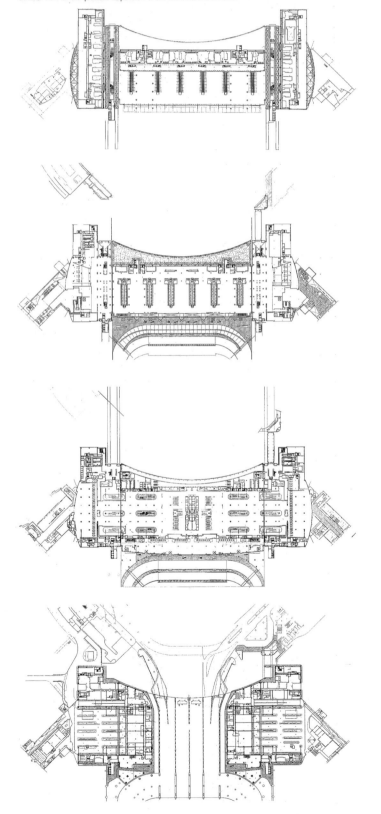

The new international terminal at San Francisco International Airport is the heart of the airport's enlargement and modernization program detailed in a 1989 pilot project by Daniel, Mann, Johnson & Mendenhall (DMJM), and later carried out by the team of architects at SOM (Skidmore, Owings & Merrill) with Del Campo & Maru and Michael Willis & Associates combining their efforts on this great project.

The project resolved one of the airport's fundamental problems, lack of expansion space, by integrating services and commercial activities in a single five-story building, making possible an increase in passenger volume from 1,200 to 5,000 per hour.

The access routes and connections to the city are also important parts of the project. Entrance roads have been enlarged and improved, while a light rail network connects the terminals. The international terminal has two stations on the fourth floor, while a new BART (Bay Area Rapid Transit) station has been incorporated on the terminal's third level, along with commercial and restaurant establishments.

The nerve center of the airport, the international terminal, was created to serve heavy air traffic, but there is also an awareness of its role in the community and its function as gateway to the city. The main structure emerges as a clearly defined image of the airport, thanks to two elements: the terminal's roof structure and its façade. Both of these, clearly visible from the air as well as from the entrance roads that serve the area, provide definite visual cohesion, a powerful, iconic comment on the way San Francisco opens its doors to the world.

The lighting, heating, ventilation and air-conditioning systems are located in the boarding and check-in areas. Thus, the roof remains free of these assemblies, and maintenance costs are reduced. Two series of balanced frame structures support a third, creating a winged form which obviously alludes to the terminal's purpose. This framework is 381 feet across in the center and 151 feet at each end. It seems to float over the building. The roof structure requires few columns, contributing to the fluidity of its main space. The ethereal quality is reinforced by the façade's curtain wall, a glass-and-metal screen that diffuses sunlight, providing protection against solar rays while lighting the interior.

In fact, natural light plays a fundamental role in articulating the building's stylistic expressiveness. Well integrated, it greatly highlights the perceived lightness of the roof and reveals the character and structure of the arrival hall. These elements combine to form a rhetoric of transparency and constructive sincerity, a metaphor for the strategic pact between the representative requirements of the world's major public institutions and a high-tech architecture that meets those needs with astounding effectiveness.

Top left: Pictures of the international terminal under construction (fall 1999).

Bottom left: Detail of the winged shape of the main area

Perspective of the terminal's large departure lounge, showing the wing-like roof structure and the ample interior space

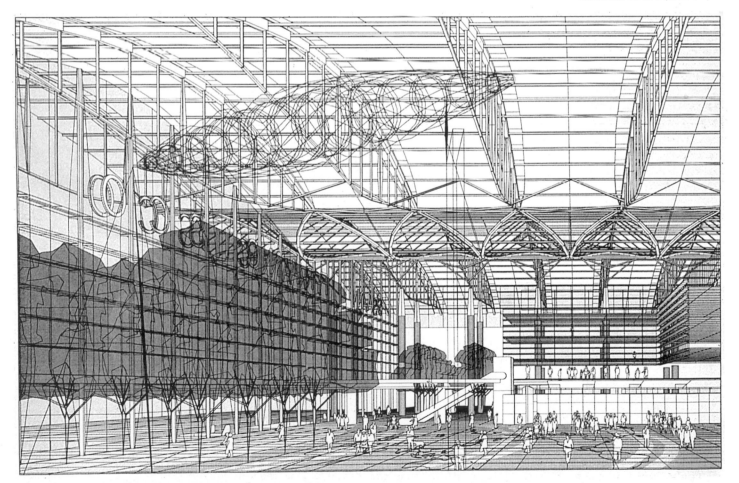

The reconfigured departures area, with six unconnected departure components incorporating ventilation and heating systems and the office block

Views of the construction of the international terminal (Fall 1999). Perspective of the façade

The main terminal building is designed to resist earthquakes expected to strike during a 1000-year period. This is currently the most demanding criterion in the United States. A fundamental decision was to place base isolators in each of the 267 columns, to stabilize the building and damp its movements in the event of an earthquake. This pendulum system allows the steel piece resting on the concave non-stick surface below it a displacement margin of 20 inches. Once the earthquake has subsided, the building's own weight helps compensate for possible displacement. This innovative damping system is complemented by the 20 inch-wide space left around the entire building to avoid damage caused to any adjacent buildings or roads by the terminal's potential sway. For example, the structures linking the terminal with the departure gates are designed to stay put during an earthquake, while the connecting elements take up any slack without difficulty

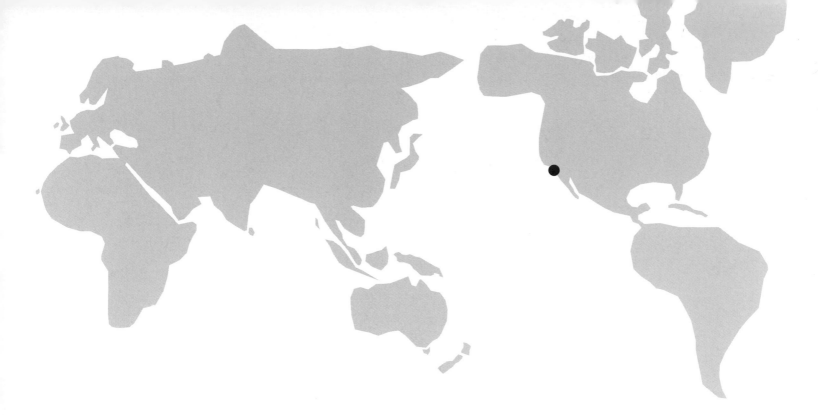

Pei Cobb Freed & Partners

SAN FRANCISCO MAIN PUBLIC LIBRARY
An emblematic building

Location **San Francisco, California, U.S.A.** Construction period **1992-1996** Client **City of San Francisco** Builder **Bureau of Construction Management and O'Brien-Kreitzberg & Associates** Structure **OLMM Structural Design** Seismic engineering **Forell/Elsesser Engineers** Photographs **Jane Lidz, Timothy Hursley** Plans **Pei Cobb Freed & Partners**

Earthquakes during the design process **Loma Prieta in 1989, 6.9 on the Richter scale, and "Northridge" in 1994, 6.7 on the Richter scale**
Initial seismic resistance of the building **Magnitude of 6.0 on the Richter scale**
Final seismic resistance (after experiencing both earthquakes) **8.3 on the Richter scale**
Seismic design **Isolation of the building's substructure**
Number of rubber isolators **144**

Floor area **374,050 sq. ft.**
Seating capacity **2,043**
Total length of shelves **37 miles**
Cost **$137,000,000**

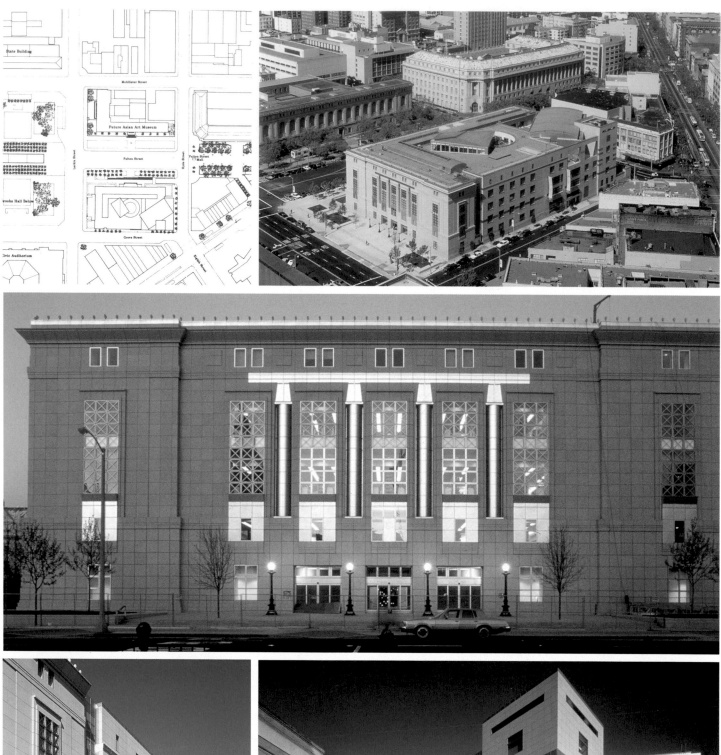

One of the principal objectives of the new San Francisco Main Public Library was to complete the configuration of the Civic Center, one of the most emblematic sites in the city, with its early and middle 20th century institutional buildings. The aim was to have the new building complement the neighborhood's historic character while presenting itself as contemporary and technologically up-to-date: a building that speaks to the past and present while looking to the future.

The project addresses this duality through a complex structure with two main elements. On Fulton and Hyde Streets, where the area's most emblematic buildings are found, a 37-foot deep, L-shaped wall was placed to contain the library's traditional component, millions of books on open shelves. Outside, this vast wall sets off the heavy materials used in the historic buildings, albeit in a somewhat non-traditional manner. The second principal material is white granite panels, approximately three square feet, that define the layout of the entire building, inside and out. This facing transforms the structure, on Grove and Larkin Streets, into an object whose steel and glass echo the commercial buildings adjacent to the library. The domed roof reinforces this connection by aligning itself with the diagonal axis of the commercial street. It therefore responds to two very different parts of the city by serving both the ceremonial and the commercial heart of San Francisco.

To optimally fit into the urban grid, this complex building required a detailed structural design in which each piece was intricately adjusted to the project's many spatial demands. Midway through the design and configuration process, following the 1989 and 1994 earthquakes, resistance requirements in the state code were made more stringent. The building can endure tremors of magnitude 8.3 on the Richter scale instead of magnitude 6.0, as originally planned. To accomplish this, the architects had to reinforce the building's substructure and superstructure. They were faced with two alternatives: increasing the size of the original structural design, thus completely upsetting the building's complicated organizational plan, or placing a shock-absorbing cushion beneath it to dissipate any potential movement of the earth. After careful study, the second option was chosen, since it would be less traumatic, less expensive, and more effective in absorbing tremors. This system, technically sophisticated, yet basically simple, provided a degree of seismic resistance found in few buildings on the California coast. The building has the same formal expression and carries on an open dialogue with each user, the multi-faceted activities of the neighborhood, and the city itself.

Approaches to these sides are dramatically announced by classical stainless steel elements that reflect the sun's rays. These reflections transform the library's white granite walls into a play of light and shadow throughout the day. This element wraps itself around the second part of the building, which is shaped by playing with the space to meet the new library's complex requirements

Detail of the Fulton Street side

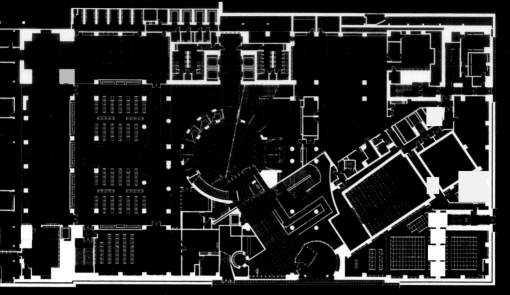

Ground floor

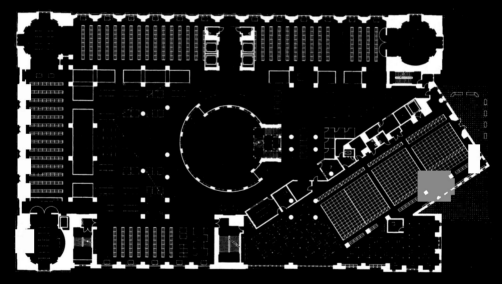

Third floor

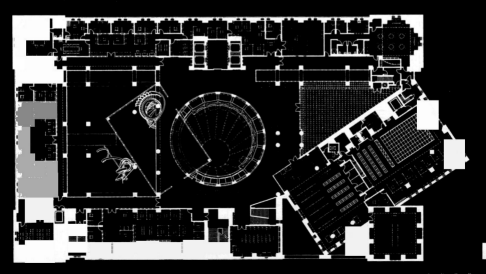

Fifth floor

N

North façade

Top left: General view of the central atrium bathed in light from the skylight

Top right: Partial view of the atrium. The stairways surround Nayland Blake's sculpture, "Constellation"

Bottom left: View of the periodicals reading room on the third floor

Bottom right: Detail of a three-story work area from the third floor

The system is comprised of 144 rubber isolators with alternating layers of steel and vulcanized rubber around a solid lead core. These shock absorbers are laid out on a four-foot concrete mat under the structural columns. This creates a cushion that isolates earth tremors while it supports the natural settling of the building

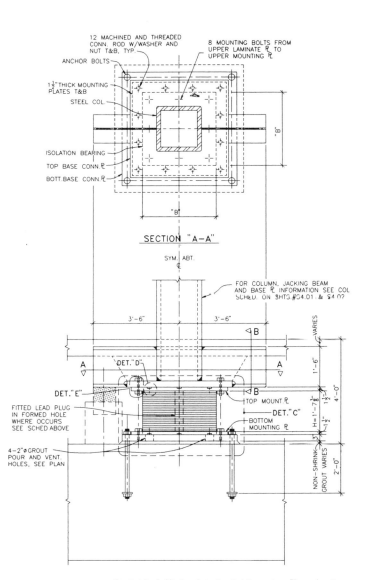

SECTION "A-A"

Detail of the building's substructure isolation system. Plan and section

Detail of isolation joint

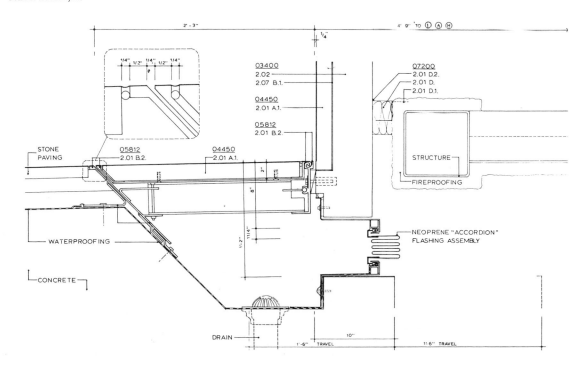

E.M. Kado & Associates

A BUSINESS CENTER; THE MONEY STORE HEADQUARTERS
Mayan images

Location **Sacramento, California, U.S.A.** Client **The Money Store Inc.** Engineering and seismic design **Marr Shaffer & Miyamoto Inc.** Contractor **Rudolph & Sletten Inc.** Steel supplier **Harrick Photos Marr Shaffer & Miyamoto Inc.**

Applicable seismic standard **Uniform Building Code (ICBO, 1994)**
Earthquakes in the area **The strongest, magnitude 6.75 on the Richter scale, occurred in 1892. Its epicenter was 25 miles west of the site**
Seismic design **Very economical viscous liquid shock absorbers**
Effect of the shock absorbers **A 60% reduction in the lateral forces affecting the foundation of the building and a 30% reduction in structural displacement. The horizontal movement of one floor with respect to the next is almost totally eliminated**
Cost of seismic design **Less than 1% of the total building cost**
Achievement **One of the first buildings constructed in the US with seismic shock absorbers**

Constructed floor space **450,473 sq. ft.**
Shape of building **Ziggurat**
Number of floors **11**
Total height: **154 ft.**
Total number of employees **2,000**
Structure **Metal frame**
Total cost **$85,000,000**

as one approaches, what from a certain distance evokes the silhouette of a Mayan temple reveals itself as a building accommodating the offices and customer services department of a finance company, The Money Store. A ziggurat shape was chosen because it provides the feeling of firmness and stability which the owners desired.

Project requirements called for an emblematic, financially viable building which in the aftermath of an earthquake could continue to operate with as little disruption as possible. Since building safety was a top priority, the structural design was of special concern. Consequently, this national and international business center is one of the first structures in the USA using seismic shock absorbers to dissipate the energy unleashed during an earthquake.

The building's structural system is a pyramid-shaped, seismic-resistant frame, occupying a square land area with 315-foot-long sides. The building steps back as it ascends; each floor is smaller than the one below, until the rectangular top level, measuring 92 by 128 feet, is reached. This effectively extends the space of each floor, permitting easy maintenance of the façades and making it possible to evacuate quickly in an emergency.

The superstructure is reinforced by a lateral system which enables the building to withstand the most critical moments of any ground shaking. The elastic, resistant frames act as braces for the post-and-lintel structure, to which viscous liquid shock absorbers have been added. This system has a clear advantage over the others which were considered. It represented only a 1% increase in the total building cost, had a much longer than expected useful life, and permitted design flexibility, since the shock absorbers can be located in any part of the framework.

Using viscous liquid shock absorbers to dissipate earth tremors reduces the structural displacement by 30% and the lateral forces substructure sustains by 60%. Horizontal displacement of one floor with respect to the next is almost totally eliminated. The seismic resistance system of the Money Store headquarters is so effective that it surpasses building code safety standards.

The end result is a highly seismic-resistant building, thanks to a design achieved at a very competitive cost, with open space permitting maximum flexibility in meeting program requirements and an impressive, glass-covered structure which appropriately reflects the image the company wishes to project.

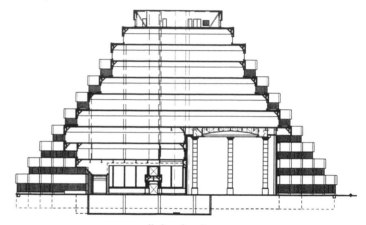

North-south section

The framework under construction

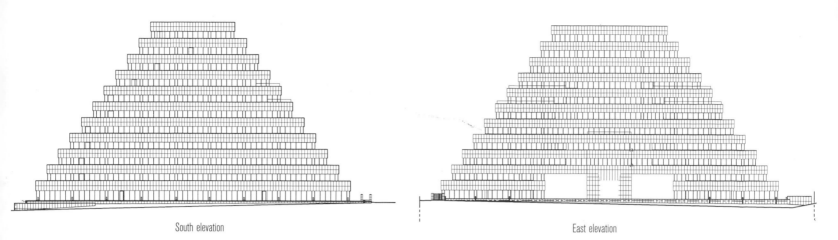

South elevation

East elevation

Structural behavior analysis in three dimensional models

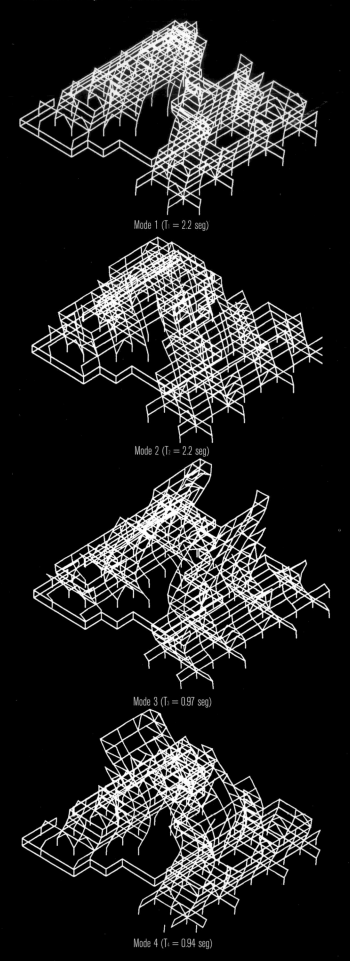

Mode 1 (T₁ = 2.2 seg)

Mode 2 (T₂ = 2.2 seg)

Mode 3 (T₃ = 0.97 seg)

Mode 4 (T₄ = 0.94 seg)

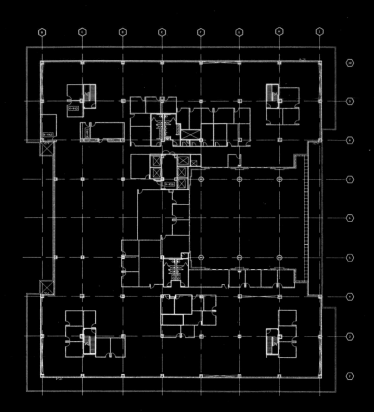

First floor

Configuration of the framework for the third floor

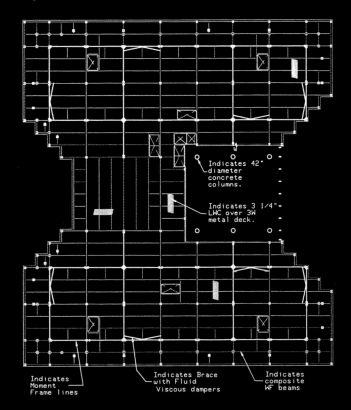

Indicates 42"
diameter
concrete
columns.

Indicates 3 1/4"
LWC over 3W
metal deck.

Indicates
Moment
Frame lines

Indicates Brace
with Fluid
Viscous dampers

Indicates
composite
WF beams

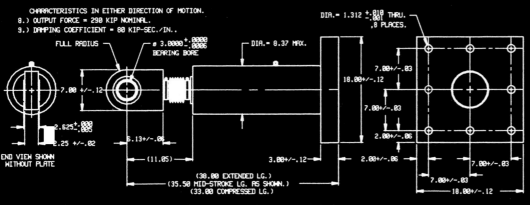

Construction detail of a seismic shock absorber

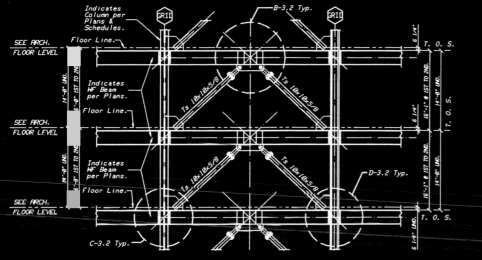

Elevation of the seismic-resistant framework with shock absorbers acting as braces

Close-up of the viscous liquid shock absorbers

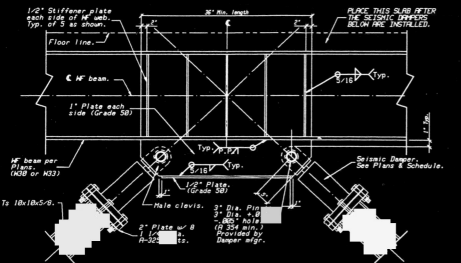

Construction detail of the shock absorber-beam connection

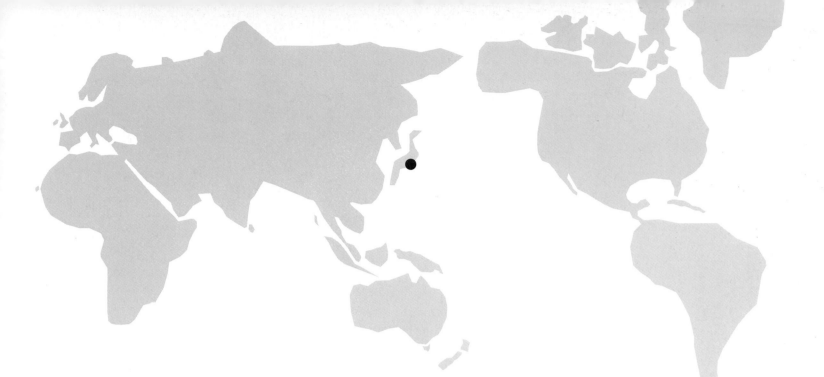

Foster & Partners

CENTURY TOWER

East and west

Location **Tokyo, Japan** Construction period **1991** Engineering **Ove Arup & Partners** Mechanical and electrical systems **J. Roger Preston & Partners** Lighting **Claude Engle** Water systems **Richard Chaix** Acoustics **Arup Acoustics and Tim Smith Acoustics** Photos and plans **Foster & Partners**

Seismic risk **Very high because Tokyo is one of the most active seismic cities in the world** Earthquake-resistant design **Strut framework**

Height **448.5 ft.**
Depth of foundation **136 ft.**
Floors, South tower **21**
Floors, North tower **19**
Total area **284,920 sq. ft.**
Total office space **117,080 sq. ft.**
Typical floor **4306 sq. ft.**

Century Tower, inaugurated on May 27, 1991 in Tokyo, Foster and Partners' first building in the Land of the Rising Sun and a major contribution to the changing architecture of the Japanese capital, sets a new standard for office ventures in that country.

Designed by the Foster and Partners studios in London and Tokyo for the Obunsha Publishing Group, the building consists of two linked towers, 19 and 21 stories high respectively. The towera are separated by a courtyard, visible from each side, which provides natural light for the center of the complex. The office floors are two-level units joined by elevators and stairs in structural cores on both sides of the tower. This arrangement is clearly exposed on the faces of the building, adding to the already striking and expressive structural framework. Apart from evoking a symbolic building image, there arc obvious practical advantages: the space is completely open.

Century Tower is located on one of the main streets of Downtown Tokyo, near a train line and next to the Bunkyo-Ku district, a historic neighborhood of small houses. The clients wanted an emblematic, distinctive building which would be a departure from Tokyo's standard commercial architecture, which, typical of so many other places, is lifeless and lacking in interest. The framework of struts gives the tower a singular appearance while meeting the demanding seismic requirements in a land where the risk of intense earthquakes and typhoons is very high.

Foster and Partners is always able to flood its buildings with natural light. The traditional luminosity of Japanese interiors made this objective even more important in this project. The courtyard is brimming with sunlight, and it improves building safety, acting as a break against fire and smoke. The first floor, a key meeting area within the complex, also enjoys direct natural light.

Besides wanting a flagship building, the designers were above all aiming for a perfect work environment. The interior design, work areas, and building systems were all created by the architectural firm. The artificial lighting and air conditioning are technologically innovative.

At the very top of the building is a residence for the client, along with a restaurant and gymnasium, under a glazed ceiling inspired by the roofs of traditional Japanese temples. The basement houses a museum where the client's art collection is displayed. The entrance to this exhibition hall is reached by a black-walled staircase behind a curtain of water. The restful effect of the water provides the perfect ambience for visitors entering the dark space, where the works of art are enhanced by direct lighting.

The project is the result of exceptional collaboration between the Japanese construction industry and international consultants. The building meets the needs of modern business and is resistant to any natural catastrophe, thanks to its integral design combining Eastern and Western values.

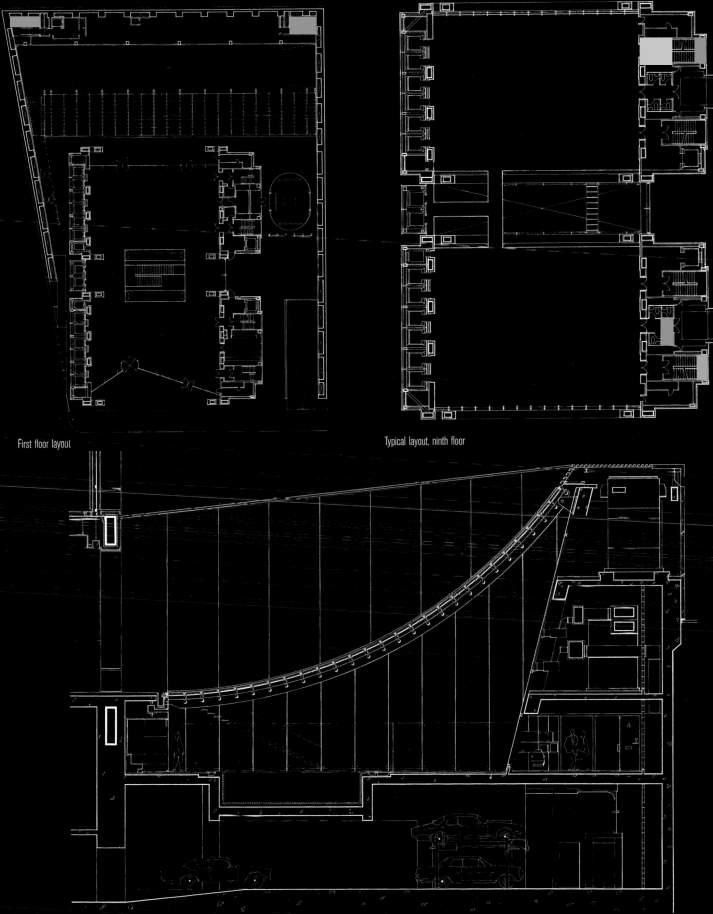

First floor layout

Typical layout, ninth floor

Axonometric perspective

Detail of an offices' floor

Foster & Partners
MILLENIUM TOWER
A vertical city

Location **Tokyo, Japan** Date of project **1990** Engineering **Ohbayashi** Photos of the model **Richard Davies, Foster & Partners**

Achivements **In 1990, the proposal to build this tower challenged what was then possible in terms of height. In fact, the Millenium Tower was to be almost twice the height of the highest building in the world at that time, the Sears Tower, and it was to be two and a half times the height of the Tokyo Tower**
Earthquake-resistant design **Top priority due to the gigantic size of the project and the high risk of earthquakes in Tokyo**

Total floor space **Nearly 11,000,000 sq. ft.**
Total height of the tower **2,627 ft.**
Height of the habitable part of the building **1,970 ft.**
Usable space **77%**
Diameter of the marina **1,313 ft.**
Diameter of the base of the tower **493 ft.**
Number of residents **50,000**
Approximate distance from dry land **1 1/4 miles**

the Japanese firm Ohbayashi, which specializes in construction and civil engineering, asked Norman Foster to investigate the implications of constructing a large-scale shopping and residential complex more than a mile from the coast. The techniques needed to build a tower in such a peculiar and incongruous location had already been explored in oil rig construction. However, the social and ecological revolution this project would represent has yet to arrive. The goal was to create an urbanistic architectural project combining various interrelated activities, work, leisure, recreation, business, and shopping, into a physical reality. The tower would be the perfect context for the ever-intensifying social, cultural, and economic changes happening in Japan today.

The plan is gargantuan: some 800 meters high with 50,000 residents. The vertical shopping center envisioned would equal all the hustle and bustle of New York's Fifth Avenue and the Champs Elysées in Paris. The diameter of the building at ground level would be 493 feet, while the marina from which it would rise would have a diameter of 1,313 feet. Obviously, a structure with these dimensions, in a high seismic risk area, requires a carefully studied structural system to guarantee stability and avoid damage during an earthquake.

The building will have an imposing appearance, but, since it is to be occupied by humans, it must also have a human scale. Accordingly, there needs to be an accessible, responsive dimension. After the initial impact when seen from across the water, the perception will be softened as one approaches and the structural elements become visible. The helical structure surrounding the skyscraper creates a shroud-like effect which integrates and unifies the bearing system with the building shape. Close-up views will reveal the articulation of the structure as a whole and the hierarchical component system. Finally, the details of the façade, entrances, and signs will herald arrival at the tower. After crossing the inhospitable sea by car, train, or ferry, visitors will have before them a structure which seems to be floating in the middle of a calm lagoon.

This strange setting will be enclosed by an enormous wall affording protection from the choppy seas and providing a venue for strolling, dining out, having a drink, shopping, fishing, or just resting while enjoying the magnificent views. A special transport system will carry people along this avenue. Inside, one will be able to take advantage of the marine recreational complex. Docks will be built for all types of ships and boats, and there will be an area with clean, calm water for swimming. At night, the lighting and reflections will embellish the seascape. Five-story "celestial centers", with open-air terraces and offering various social and leisure activities, such as restaurants, gymnasiums, cinemas, and auditoriums, will be distributed the entire height of the building.

The maritime recreational facilities will be accessible over bridges from the train and ferry stations. The tower's spacious entrance will occupy six floors: three above the arrival level, including the lobby, reception, and elevators, and three below, with shops, restaurants, and bars accented by patios and skylights for natural illumination.

These leisure areas will be connected by escalators. On the south side, a large plaza will offer views of the marina. All these attractions will be available to both project residents and visitors and tourists

The base of the model

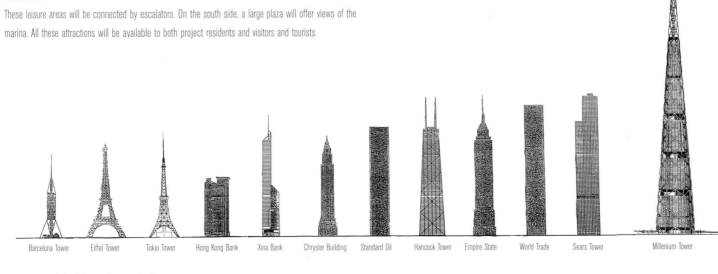

| Barcelona Tower | Eiffel Tower | Tokio Tower | Hong Kong Bank | Xina Bank | Chrysler Building | Standard Oil | Hancock Tower | Empire State | World Trade | Sears Tower | Millenium Tower |

A comparison of the Millenium Tower and other towers

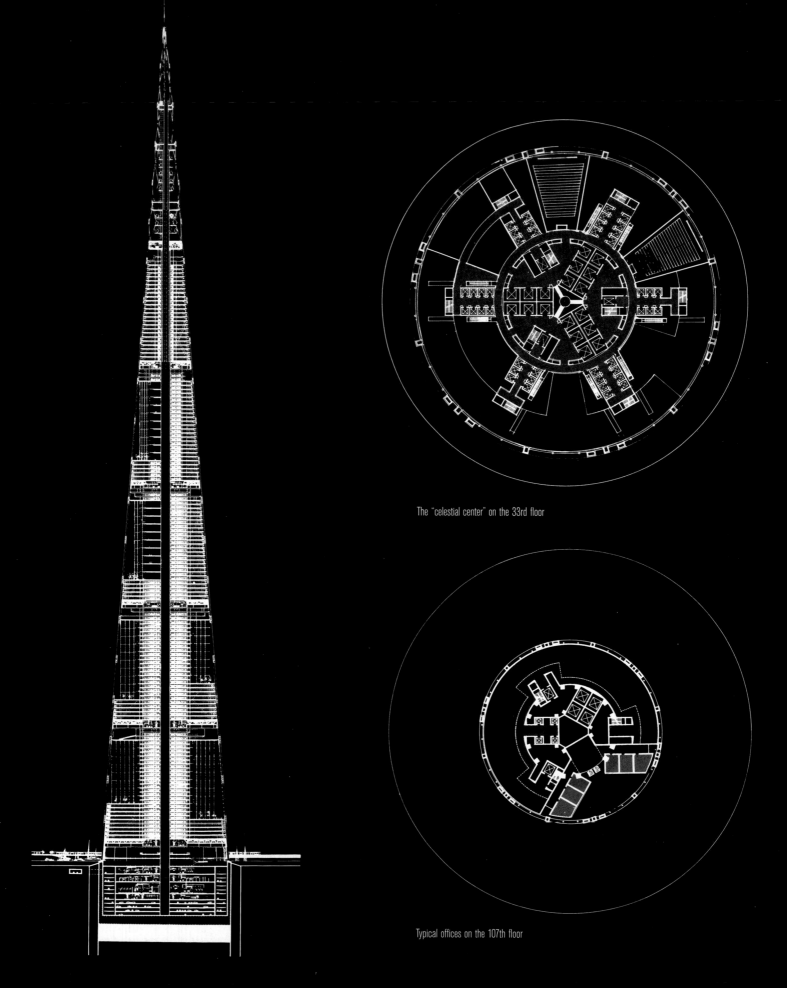

The "celestial center" on the 33rd floor

Typical offices on the 107th floor

Cross section

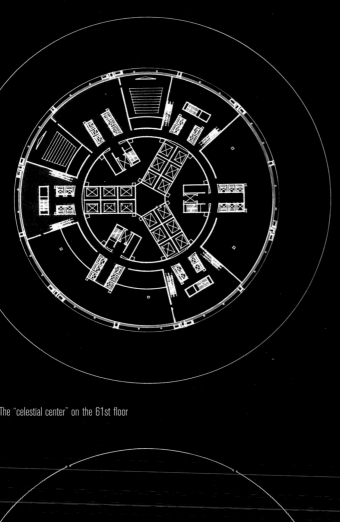

The "celestial center" on the 61st floor

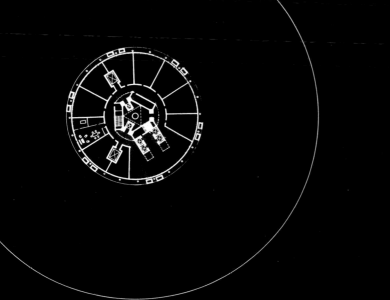

Typical offices on the 137th floor

Itsuko Hasegawa Atelier
THE FRUIT MUSEUM
Technological filigree

Location **Yamanashi, Japan** Construction period **1992-1995** Clients **Yamanashi Prefect** Engineers **Ovc Arup & Partners Japan Ltd.** Installations **Setsuhi Keikaku** Contractor **Fujita Corporation** Photography **Hidoki Nishizawa, Mitsumasa Fujitsuka, Itsuko Hasegawa, Tomio Ohashi, Taisuke Ogawa and KIAC**

Relationship to earthquakes **It is located 18 miles from Mount Fuji, in one of the most active seismic zones in the world** Program used for the structural calculations of the three main buildings **Oasys DYNA3D**

Number of buildings **3**
Roof form **Dome**
Largest dome **165 ft. wide by 65 ft. high**

General view

1. Plaza
2. Exhibition hall
3. Tropical greenhouse
4. Workshop
5. Bridge
6. Small greenhouse
7. Aquatic garden
8. Information point
9. Leaf House (administration)

Above: View of the complex
Left: The plaza under construction
Lower left: The dome containing the greenhouse
Lower right: Detail of the east façade of the greenhouse

Above left: Building where conferences on such topics as fruit preparation methods are held
Above right: West façade of the workshop

the Fruit Museum is located in the city of Yamanashi, 18 miles from 12,400-foot Mount Fuji. This area is one of the principal fruit-growing regions in Japan and one of the most seismically active zones in the world.

As its name implies, the museum, part of a public park, is dedicated to the subject of fruit. It concerns itself with this humble topic from numerous points of view, both specific, such as aesthetics and religious significance, and more general, including the environment and human beings' relationship to fruit (sensuality, desire, etc.). Thus, the project is a poetic manifestation of the many aspects that are addressed.

Three separate domes housing the plaza, the tropical greenhouse, and the workshop, comprise the museum. The setting is garden-like. The first two structures are joined below ground by an exhibition space. In the plaza, visitors can taste drinks made from different fruits. In the greenhouse, different species of tropical plants from all over the planet are cultivated. The workshop is the scene of conferences on fruits and classes on different ways to prepare them.

The domes, despite their large dimensions (the largest is 165 feet wide and 65 feet high) and their foundations, seem as if they have just landed or are on the point of taking off. The buildings' apparent weightlessness relates to the project's symbolism, whereby the different structures are simple metaphors for a few scattered seeds or, going even further, a representation of the fertility and vitality associated with fruit.

The skillful Ove Arup engineering is, as always, in evidence in the Fruit Museum. Because of the high seismic risk, an exhaustive analysis of the domes' tubular steel structures was carried out in order to ensure appropriate behavior during potential earth movement. The results showed that the design conditions under seismic loading were more severe than under wind pressures.

During the project phase, Arup was unsure about whether the usual comparative structural model analyses under earthquake acceleration were sufficient to define the masses needed for the museum. Consequently, the Oasys DYNA3D computer program was employed to calculate each of the three geodesic dome structures separately. Each was analyzed in three different ways: statically, dynamically, and in terms of sensitivity to warping. This was a major step forward for Oasys, as it was the program's first real test.

Itsuko Hasegawa perfects a nuance-filled plan with relative simplicity while uniting seemingly irreconcilable concepts like past, present, and future; indigenous and global environments; and the natural and the artificial.

View of the plaza through the greenhouse structure

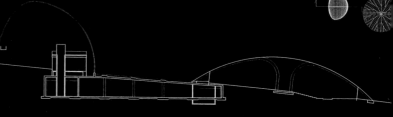

Cross section (above) and ground plan (below) of the tropical greenhouse and the plaza, connected at basement level by an exhibition hall

Night view of the east façade of the greenhouse

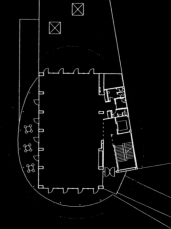

Interior of the workshop's third floor

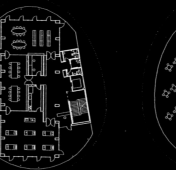

Workshop. Ground and first floor (above) and second floor, third floor, and roof (above)

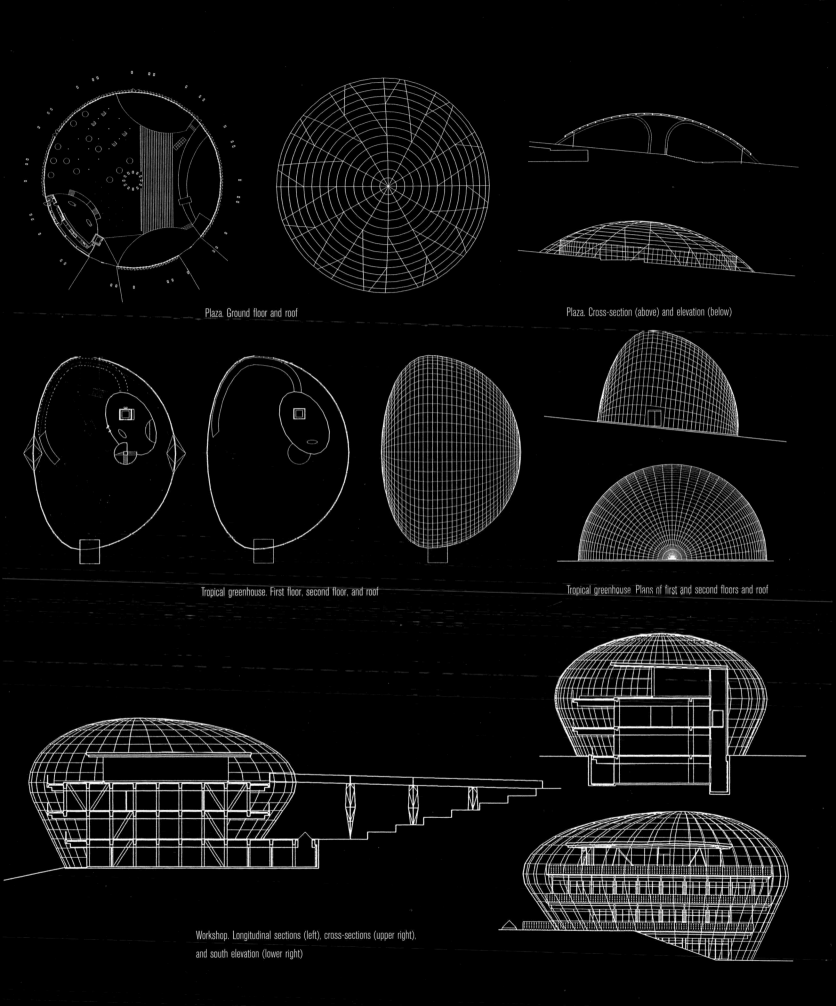

Plaza. Ground floor and roof

Plaza. Cross-section (above) and elevation (below)

Tropical greenhouse. First floor, second floor, and roof

Tropical greenhouse. Plans of first and second floors and roof

Workshop. Longitudinal sections (left), cross-sections (upper right),
and south elevation (lower right)

HSBA-Honshu Shikoku Bridge Authority
AKASHI-KAIKYO BRIDGE
Longest suspension bridge in the world

Location **Kobe, Japan** Construction period **1994-1998** Photography **Honshu Shikoku Bridge Authority**

Earthquake history **"Hanshin" earthquake, January 17, 1995, magnitude of 7.2 on the Richter scale**
Status of the bridge on January 17, 1995 **Under construction**
Structural damage **None, although some components were moved nearly three feet**
Seismic risk **The seismically active Nojima fault is very close to the bridge**
Maximum seismic resistance **Magnitude of 8.5 on the Richter scale**
Seismic recurrence period **150 years**
Wind resistance **78 miles/second**

Function **Connects Kobe to the island of Awajishima**
Total bridge length **2.43 miles**
Central span **1.24 miles**
Achievement **Largest suspension bridge in the world**
Tower height **975 ft. above sea level**
Maximum water depth **360 ft.**
Number of highway lanes **6**
Amount of steel in the superstructure **193,000 tons**
Amount of concrete in the superstructure **15 million sq. ft.**

three routes connect Honshu and Shikoku, two of the four largest islands in Japan, by a series of bridges and viaducts joining smaller islands along the paths. At one end of the easternmost route, which links the densely populated city of Kobe with the much smaller Naruto, is the Akashi-Kaikyo Bridge.

The idea of connecting Honshu and Shikoku was far from new. Travel between the islands was unsafe, essentially because of harsh weather conditions and the high rate of natural disasters (volcanoes, earthquakes, typhoons, and tsunamis). This made the idea of joining the islands with assured, secure connections an attractive one throughout the 20th Century. However, it did not become a reality until the dawn of the 21st Century.

In April 1998, the Akashi-Kaikyo Bridge, the longest suspension bridge in the world, was opened to traffic. It crosses one of the most famous straits in the world, with the heaviest maritime traffic in Japan, connecting Osaka Bay with the Harima Gulf.

Design of the infrastructure had to take into account the fact that the area had suffered several earthquakes, the largest of which measured 6 on the Richter scale. In addition, the complicated orography in the strait required anchoring one of the towers of the bridge's central span on a steep slope, while the other foundation was relatively flat. The enormous wind forces, moreover, were especially relevant, as they are for all suspension bridges, because of their flexibility. In fact, the abundance of typhoons clearly made in-depth climatological studies necessary. To examine these factors and investigate potential design criteria applicable to an area with such extreme conditions, an observation tower was built in 1964 near the future site of the bridge.

Starting in 1977, general seismic design parameters were established for bridges between Honshu and Shikoku. These were applicable, primarily, to structures with foundations on granite. For the Akashi-Kaikyo Bridge, whose enormous foundations would have to be built on less solid ground, an alternate formula was needed. The bridge was built to allow for oscillation, but with a combination of rigid and flexible elements which resulted in a very low natural frequency. In practice, the force of the wind and the effects of any earthquakes should be absorbed by the structure and barely perceptible on the bridge highway.

The Akashi-Kaikyo Bridge seismic design was put to the test during construction by the intense earthquake that shook the area on January 17, 1995. Originating on the Nojima fault, which passes directly under the central span of the bridge, the tremors only slightly displaced that section.

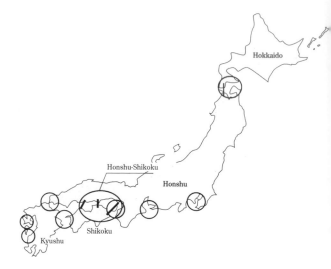

Connections (existing and proposed) between Japanese islands

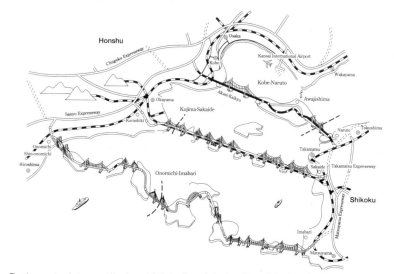

The three routes that connect Honshu and Shikoku: Oromichi-Imabari, Kojima-Sakaide, and Kobe-Naruto. The latter includes the Akashi-Kaikyo Bridge

General aerial view from the Island of Honshu

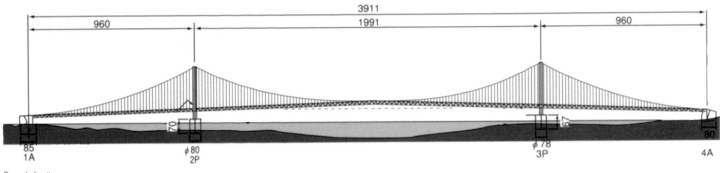

General elevation

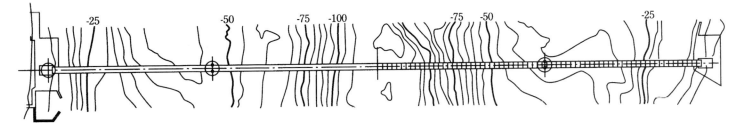

General plan

Front and side elevation of one of the towers

View from the shore

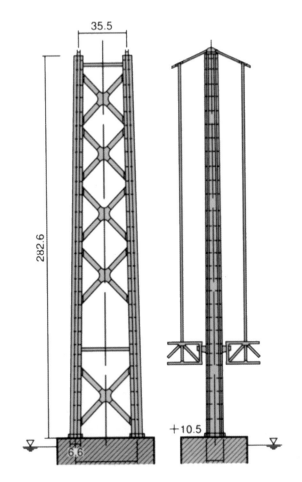

View of the bridge at night

Top to bottom: Towing one of the
caissons, anchoring and cabling,
and a girder forming the platform
for the highway

1

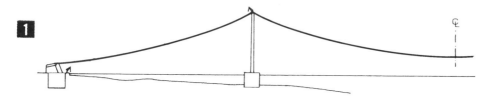

2

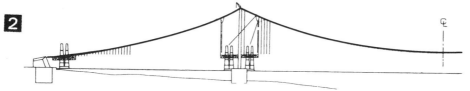

3

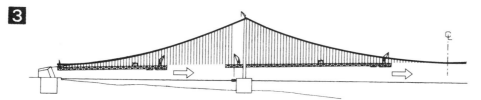

4

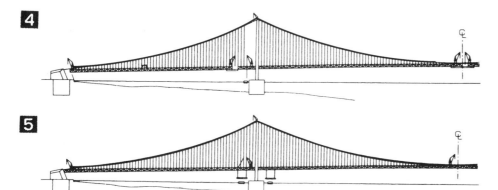

5

Different phases of girder construction

View of the bridge and highway from the top of one of the towers

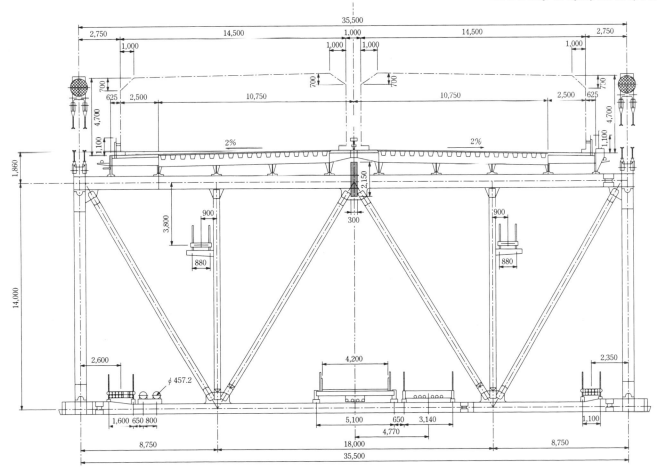

Cross section of the platform

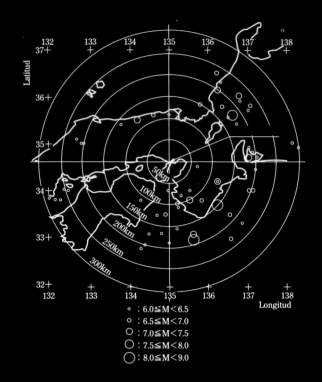

o : 6.0≦M<6.5
o : 6.5≦M<7.0
O : 7.0≦M<7.5
◯ : 7.5≦M<8.0
◯ : 8.0≦M<9.0

When the earthquake struck, the Akashi-Kaikyo Bridge was still under construction. The two towers had been positioned and the cables had been pulled, but platform construction had yet to begin. Detailed examination of the structure showed that its components had suffered no damage. However, the four foundations were displaced by the tremors. The central span was extended by approximately two and a half feet and one of the lateral spans was extended by one foot. The three and a half foot increase in total length moved the cables upward approximately four feet

Earthquakes recorded from 1885 to 1979: epicenters and magnitudes

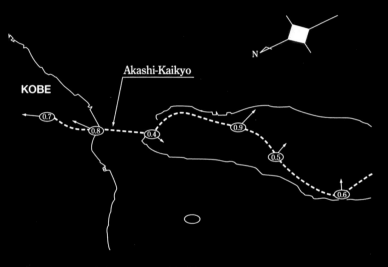

Study of earth crust displacement on part of the Kobe-Naruto route after the January 17, 1995, earthquake

Accelerations in the area. The peak was registered in the January 17, 1995, Kobe earthquake

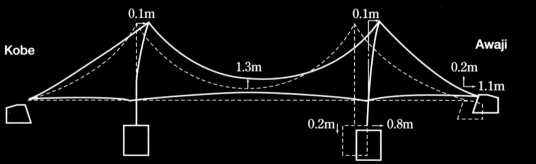

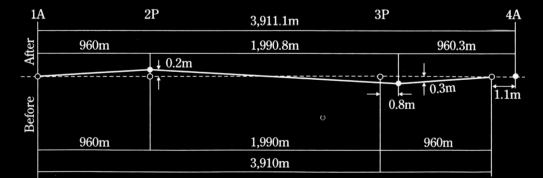

Study of the relative deformation of the Akashi-Kaikyo Bridge after the Kobe earthquake. Plan and elevation

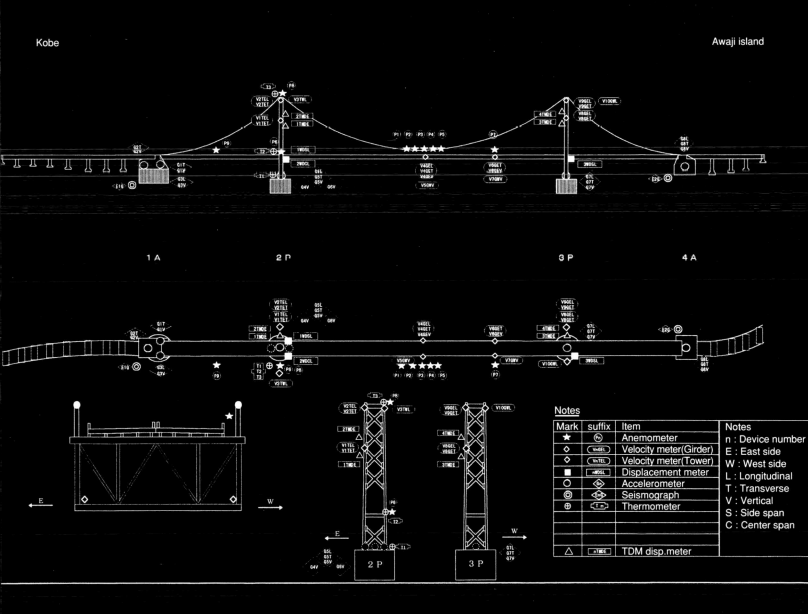

an showing the arrangement of climatological and
ismic control devices on the Akashi-Kaikyo Bridge

Rotation of a universal joint

Kobe

Awaji island

1 A   2 P   3 P   4 A

Notes

Mark	suffix	Item
★	Pn	Anemometer
◇	VnGEL	Velocity meter(Girder)
◇	VnTEL	Velocity meter(Tower)
■	nWDSL	Displacement meter
○	An	Accelerometer
◎	Enn	Seismograph
⊕	T n	Thermometer
△	nTMDE	TDM disp.meter

Notes

n : Device number
E : East side
W : West side
L : Longitudinal
T : Transverse
V : Vertical
S : Side span
C : Center span

Shigeru Ban
TEMPORARY HOUSING FOR PEOPLE AFFECTED BY THE KOBE EARTHQUAKE
Recyclable dwellings

Location **Nagata-ku, Kobe, Japan** Construction date **1995** Clients **Vietnamese refugees left homeless after the earthquake** Structure **Sho Tezuka** Collaborators **TSP Taiyo** Photographs **Hiroyuki Hiral**

Relationship to earthquakes **Constructed after the "Hanshin" earthquake (1994, Kobe, Japan, magnitude of 7.2 on the Richter scale)**
Manual labor **Vietnamese and Japanese volunteers**

Dwelling size **172 sq. ft. (the same dimensions as the basic UNCHR dwelling for Rwanda)**
Structure **Paper tubes**
Diameter of paper tubes **4 1/4 inches**
Thickness of paper tubes **.16 inches**
Price of dwelling unit **Very low cost ($1,270)**
Number of dwellings built initially **21**

most research on seismic architecture centers around the need to make buildings more resistant and able to withstand earthquake tremors by applying ever more sophisticated technologies which generally represent a significant portion of the project's budget. The research promoted by Japanese architect Shigeru Ban on buildings made from paper tubes has made it possible to develop very low cost dwellings that are easy to construct. These units, created for use in the wake of disasters, are more versatile than the traditional tents and, moreover, greatly improve refugee living conditions.

After the Great Hanshin earthquake, which measured 7.2 on the Richter scale, Kobe politicians promised to rapidly provide temporary housing for the victims. However, some months later, many were still living in plastic tents and others were totally without shelter, because they had to remain in the area of their workplaces and schools. In response, Shigeru Ban quickly developed the design for a paper house and produced a prototype which he built with his own hands and without using a single sophisticated tool.

The design criterion was an inexpensive structure that could be built by anyone, with reasonable amounts of light and ventilation and an at least acceptable appearance. The solution was a 172-square-foot module on a foundation of sand-filled beer crates, with walls of paper tubes 4 1/4 mm in diameter and 4 mm (.16") thick, and a waterproof roof. The beer crates, rented from the local manufacturer, were also used as stairs during the construction process. Self-adhesive waterproof tape was applied in the space between the paper tubes. The roofing material is not attached to the tubular elements so that the ends can remain open, to provide ventilation in summer, or closed off, to conserve warm air in winter. The total cost of each unit, considering the savings in material transport and storage, is extremely low.

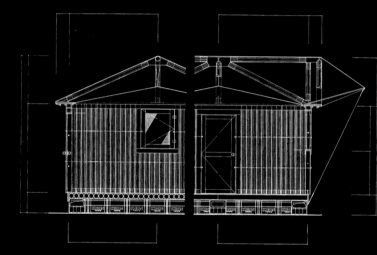

Section

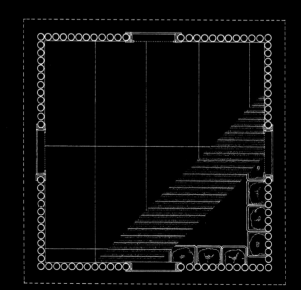

Floor

The paper house offers enormous advantages, since each element can be reused and does not require a great deal of pre-planned storage. All that is needed is an instruction manual since, as in the case of Rwanda, the paper tubes can be manufactured on site

Ban's work for the Kobe community is particularly important since it embraces the idea of community participation. He rejects the deep-rooted parochial concept of the land in favor of a new, much broader concept of applied architecture, radically redefining the profession's parameters in Japan

In comparison with traditional tents, in which summer temperatures can reach 104 degrees Fahrenheit and water can flood the interior, these temporary units provide optimum hygiene and living standards. Their size and the way they can be situated to provide shade makes the area appear more like a small town than a camp

Renzo Piano Building Workshop
KANSAI INTERNATIONAL AIRPORT
An island in the sea

Location **Osaka Bay, Kansai, Japan** Construction period **1988-1994** Client **Kansai International Airport Co. Ltd.** Co-executors **N.Okabe, in association with Nikken Sekkei Ltd., Paris Airports, Japan Airport Consultants Inc.** Sculptor **Shingu** Photographs **Yoshio Hata, Kanji Hiwatashi, S. Ishida, E. Minetti, Gianni Berengo Gardin, Skyfront, Kitajima, Kinumaki**
Contest, 1988 Project **J. F. Blassel, R. Brennan, A. Chaaya, L. Couton, R. Keiser, L. Koenig, K. McBryde, S. Planchez, R. Rolland, G. Torre, O. Touraine with G. le Breton, M. Henry, J. Lelay, A. O'Carroll, M. Salerno, A.H. Téménidès, N. Westphal** Structure and building systems **Ove Arup & Partners** Landscape Gardening **M.Desvigne**
Basic project and detail, 1989-1991 Project **J. F. Bassel, A. Chavela, I. Corte, K. Fraser, R. S. Garlipp, M. Goerd, G. Hall, K. Hirano, A. Ikegami, S. Ishida, A. Johnson, C. Kelly, T. Kimura, S. Larsen, J. Lelay, K. McBryde, T. Miyazaki, S. Nakaya, N. Takata, T. Tomuro, O. Touraine, M. Turpin, M. Yamada, H. Yamaguchi, T. Yamaguchi with A. Autin, G. Cohen, A. Golzari, B. Gunning, G. Hastrich, M. Horie, I. Kubo, S. Medio, K. Miyake, S. Montaldo, S. Mukai, K. A. Naderi, S. Oehler, T. O'Sullivan, P. Persia, F. Randrei, M. Rossato, R. Shields, T. Takagawa, T. Ueno, K. Uezono, J. M. Weill, T. Yamakoshi** Structure and building systems **Ove Arup & Partners** Acoustics **Peutz & Associés** Facades **R. J. Van Santen** Cost control **David Langson & Everest, Futaba Quantity Surveying Co. Ltd.** Landscape Gardening **K. Nyunt** Construction, 1991-1994 Project **A. Ikegami, T. Kimura, T. Tomuro, Y. Ueno with S. Kano, A. Shimizu** Facades **RFR** Canyon **Toshi Keikan Sekkei Inc.**

Standard to be met **The Building Standard Law of Japan (BSLJ), one of the strictest in the world**
Earthquakes suffered **The "Hanshin" (Kobe), January 17, 1995**
Number of deaths caused by the earthquake **4,000**
Magnitude of the earthquake **7.2 on the Richter scale**
Depth of the epicenter **18 miles (below Awajishima Island)**
Distance of the airport from the epicenter **28 miles**
Earthquake damage to the island **Light settling at some spots on the perimeter**
Damage to the building from the earthquake **None**

Surface of the man-made island **5.8 sq. miles**
Total surface of the airport **91 acres**
Daily capacity **100,000 passengers**
Annual capacity **25,000,000 passengers**
Total length of building **Slightly more than one mile**
Number of boarding gates **42**
Roof surface area **968,760 sq. ft.**
Number of stainless steel panels **82,000**
Duration of construction **38 months**
Total estimated cost **$2,000,000**
Number of workers **6,000 (variable, up to 10,000)**

this airport was built on a man-made island constructed to make up for the lack of space on land. As it is three miles from Osaka Bay, the effects of noise pollution are minimized and the airport can therefore remain open twenty-four hours a day. On a busy route, it is a hub which principally serves three cities in the Kansai region: Osaka, Kobe, and Kyoto.

This man-made island, an extraordinary work of civil engineering, is built on more than a thousand piles in unstable terrain. The piles pass through 65 feet of water and as much mud, and are anchored in 130 feet of rock. To compensate for the constant movement of the mud layer, a system of sensors warns when a pile shifts more than the acceptable four tenths of an inch. Each pile has its own calibration system which readjusts the depth using powerful hydraulic jacks. After the airport has been operating for ten years, the piles can be secured permanently.

The Kansai terminal was intended to operate in an extraordinarily precise manner. It had to meet extremely demanding technical requirements both because of the strict standards for dealing with earthquakes and tsunamis and because of the enormous daily passenger volume. Certain key design features, such as the aerodynamic styling of the roof, the airport's principal innovation, were made possible only through computer technology.

The shape of the roof in cross section, an undulating, irregular arc made up of a series of different-sized arcs, resulted from the study of air currents flowing through the building. They are channeled, following the shape of the roof, through the passenger area out onto the runway, and do not require any enclosed air vents. Mobiles created by the sculptor Shingu bear witness to the ceaseless movement of the air currents.

Seismographs were placed on the ground floor and on the roof of the airport to provide firsthand information and measurements in connection with earthquakes, and to study the effects of vertical and horizontal acceleration on the airport. The first conclusions indicated that the 7.2 Richter scale earthquake that shook the Kobe area in 1995, the "Hanshin", could be considered, according to the parameters applied in Japan, below level one.

The Japanese standards, among the strictest in the world, envision two possible seismic situations. A level one refers to earthquakes of an intensity that will probably occur once in the life of the building. The building structures are designed to prevent significant damage and continue functioning without difficulty. In contrast, a level two refers to earthquakes so severe that they could even bring the building down.

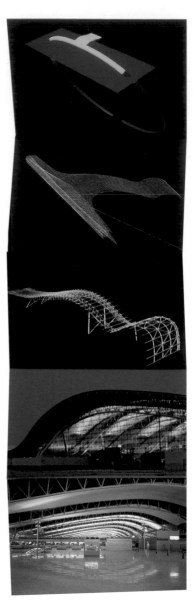

The general structure of the building is reminiscent of a wave. Its shape fits in perfectly with the immediate surroundings: the movement of the water, the wind, the sea breeze, the clarity of the light

General elevation

Ground plan

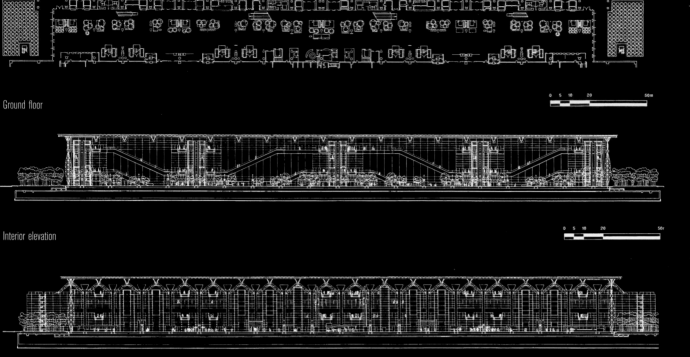

Ground floor

0 5 10 20 50m

Interior elevation

0 5 10 20 50r

Interior elevation

0 5 10 20

The organization of the terminal is based on studies conducted by Paul Andreu for Aéroports de Paris. The main section, higher on the side that overlooks the runways, handles the passengers and guides them to their correct destinations. It is linked with its two adjacent wings through a shuttle. Wherever the users are in the complex, the asymmetrical shape helps them orient themselves so they can make connections rapidly

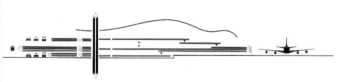

Circulation plan

Each of the four levels has a specific function. Starting from the first floor, we find international arrivals, domestic flight departures and arrivals, the shopping area and restaurants, and finally, international departures

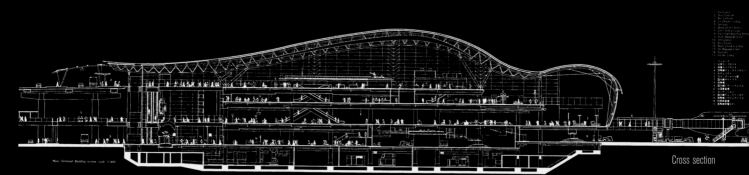

Cross section

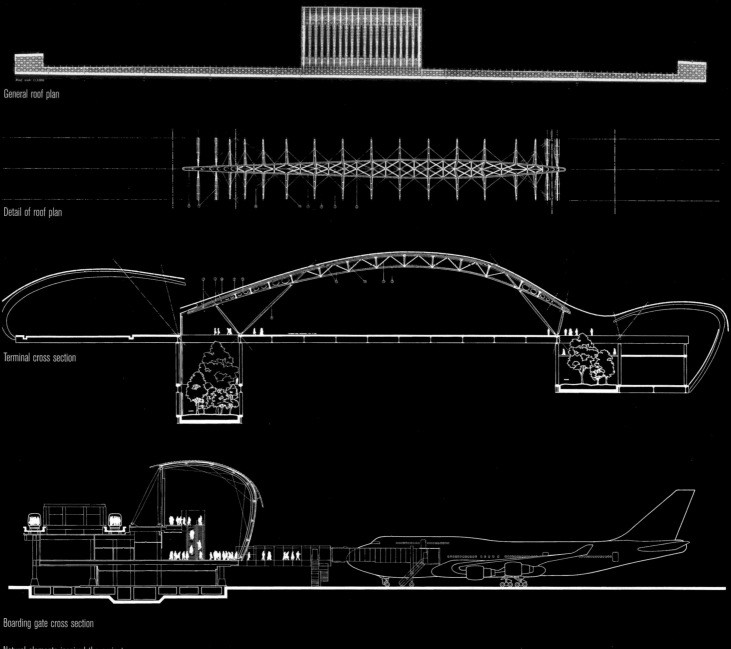

General roof plan

Detail of roof plan

Terminal cross section

Boarding gate cross section

Natural elements inspired the project
and have been incorporated into it. An
example is the indoor garden with
trees bathed in sunlight and visible
from all levels

All the building systems are near ground level to minimize the weight on each floor. In addition, the tree-shaped supporting structure has been used for lighting, loudspeakers, and video screens

B A B

66.7°

RADIUS 16.62 km

Construction detail. Various elements seen from inside and outside during the construction phase

Load distribution under normal conditions

Load distribution under earthquake conditions

The light, fluid structure of the airport does not sacrifice any resistance. Indeed, although Kansai was as close to the epicenter as Kobe, and experienced tremors of the same intensity, when the 1995 quake was over it was clear that Renzo Piano's building had emerged unscathed. "The fury of the elements toppled the oak but did not break the light, flexible reed".
Renzo Piano

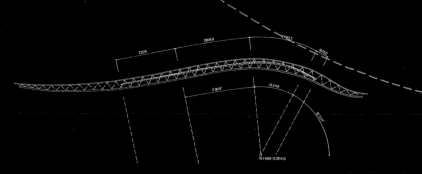

System which maintains the building in a horizontal position

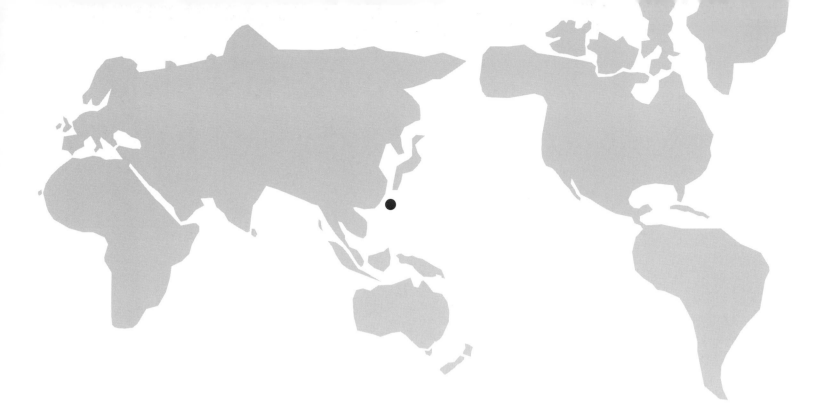

Artech Inc.

THE CEC BUILDING
The structure: beginning and end

Location **Taipei, Taiwan** Date of construction **1999** Client **Continental Engineering Corporation Inc.** Engineering **Ove Arup & Partners (Los Angeles), Supertech Engineering Consultants and Paul Chen**
Photos **King-Le Chang and Scott Hudgins**

Earthquakes suffered **"Chi-Chi" on September 21, 1999**
Earthquake magnitude **7.6 on the Richter scale**
Earthquake damage **None**
Applicable seismic standard **Taiwan building code**
Earthquake risk in Taipei **High, because the land is
sedimentary and not very compact. There is a long
vibration period**
Maximum ground acceleration **0.23 g**
Expected period between earthquakes **475 years**

Constructed floor space **189,145 sq. ft.**
Total height **197 ft.**
Number of floors above ground **13**
Number of floors below ground **4**

the Continental Engineering Corporation (CEC) headquarters, in the financial center of Taipei, provide a new architectural reference on the urban downtown scene. The building, which houses the offices of one of Taiwan's biggest construction companies, is 197 feet high with thirteen floors, including two devoted to boardrooms. In addition, there are four underground levels containing the mechanical systems and parking area.

This project had four key objectives: first, an exterior anti-seismic design which would keep the interior free of columns; second, a structure rigid enough in the face of torsion forces to enhance response during any telluric movements; third, a structure with unique style and functionality; and finally, a structure which would optimize the building site within code limitations.

The basin in which the city of Taipei is located is a high-risk earthquake zone according to the Taiwanese standards. The catastrophic consequences of earthquakes in this region result mainly from the rather loose, sedimentary soil, which has a long vibration period and a tendency to magnify the earth tremors in layers near the surface.

Understandably, therefore, one of the main concerns of the project was to ensure resistance during earthquakes. To achieve this end, the weight distribution on each floor was made as symmetrical as possible. In addition, two complementary structural elements were combined to ensure dissipation of the energy unleashed by the earthquake. From the third floor up, the system of corner struts, designed only to support their own weight, absorbs the tension generated after seismic movements, while reinforced concrete porticos at the base of the building transfer this energy from the third floor to the ground. Moreover, the corner struts are connected via beams, which respond elastically to any overload in the system, to the columns that run the entire height of the building. It is anticipated that, in the event of an extremely intense earthquake, the damage suffered by the structural system would be concentrated in these connection beams, twisting them due to their ductility and capacity to absorb energy.

The complex structural system was placed on the perimeter of each floor to avoid columns and office-space dividers, and to maximize the utility and flexibility of the space.

The clients wanted the building to reflect the spirit of the construction company and be an emblematic edifice for the capital. Without question, the efficient structural anti-seismic system makes the building an easily recognizable symbol of the corporate image. Outside the tower's glass skin, the columns, metal beams, and system of braces and struts on the corners produce a singular and distinctive overall effect.

The building responded in an exemplary fashion to the earthquake which struck Taipei on September 21, 1999, measuring 7.6 on the Richter scale. The CEC building was not damaged.

Strut systems similar to the one installed on the CEC building have been used many times in buildings with metal frameworks, because of their high earthquake resistance. This, combined with porticos able to withstand strong movements, achieves an optimal anti-seismic structural system of moderate weight.

The building responded perfectly to the earthquake which struck Taipei on September 21, 1999, measuring 7.6 on the Richter scale. The CEC headquarters was not damaged

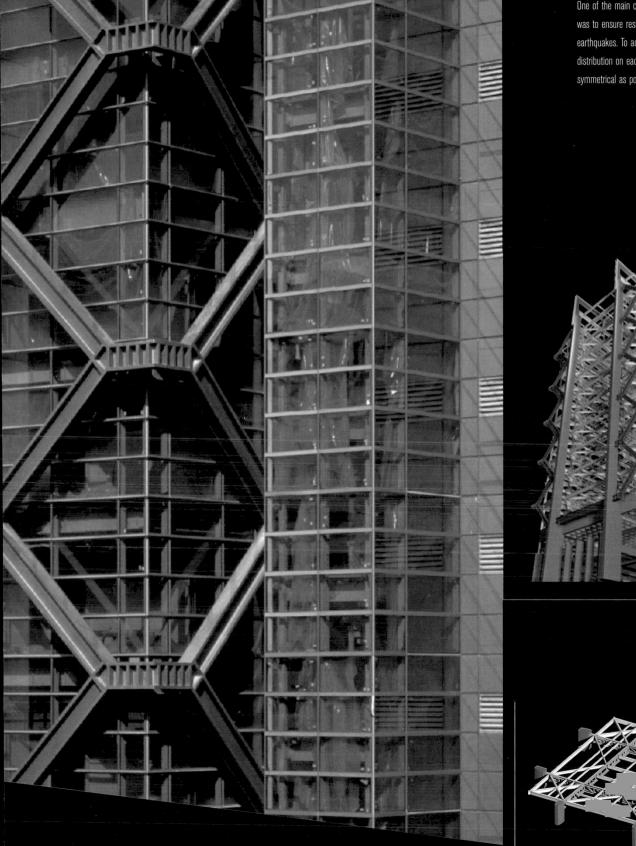

One of the main concerns of the project was to ensure resistance during earthquakes. To achieve this, the weight distribution on each floor was made as symmetrical as possible

Structural scheme of the first floor

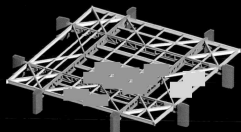

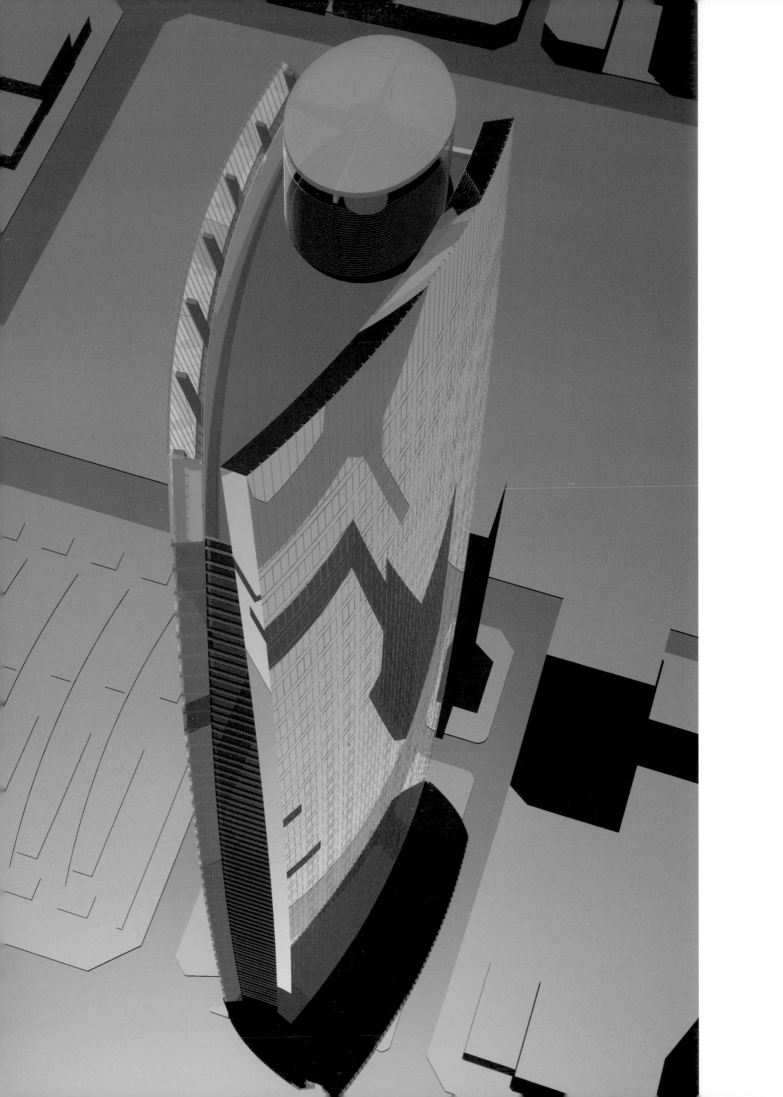

KPF-Kohn Pedersen Fox Associates PC

TAICHUNG TOWER II
Earthquake-resistant

Associate Architects **Chang & Jan. Architects & Planners** Location **Taichung, Taiwan** Construction period **1996-2000** Client **Tzung Tang Development Group Co. Ltd.** Structure **Federal Engineering Consultants Ltd.**

Earthquakes suffered **"Chi-Chi," September 21, 1999, magnitude of 7.3 on the Richter scale**
Fault on which the earthquake originated **Chelungpu**
Earthquake damage **Still under construction (installation of the curtain wall had begun), the building suffered no damage**
Maximum ground acceleration for Taichung Tower II **0.23 g**
Expected recurrence **475 years**
Building resistance **Level IX on the Mercalli scale**

Site area **24,750 sq. ft.**
Building area **12,375 sq. ft.**
Numbers of floors **47**
Numbers of floors below ground **6**
Building height from street to roof **578 ft.**
Uses **Hotel, restaurant, offices, parking**
Numbers of hotel rooms **300**

aichung Tower II is located on a rise in the city of Taichung, at the foot of a one kilometer long park area. However, the tower's design was inspired not only by the specifics of the site, but also by the mysticism and symbolism in the culture.

The plan progressively took on the outline of a fish. In researching the calligraphic origins of Chinese symbols, the image of a fish facing east was found to be regarded in Taiwan as a sign of good luck. From the moment of that discovery, the project focused on a configuration which would reinforce this initial resemblance in general as well as in the structural details.

The sculpted shape of Taichung Tower II results from the curvature–in ground plan as well as elevation–of the skin which is progressively adjusted to the reduced size of each story as the height increases. Floor-to-floor access and service areas are concentrated on the west side of each story, opening the building up to views of the park. The result is a shape with poetic simplicity whose unusual contour establishes the building's position in the city.

Taiwan experienced several major earthquakes in the 20th century. The last of these, magnitude 7.3 on the Richter scale, awakened the city of Taichung on September 21, 1999, with its tremors. The epicenter of "Chi-Chi," as it was called, was in the island's central mountains. It originated on the Chelungpu fault, which was believed to be largely inactive. "Chi-Chi's" strong tremors caused surface cracks, landslides, and liquefaction.

After the earthquake, it was noted that high buildings–and, in general, reinforced concrete more than metal structures–were especially vulnerable to the tremors. In some cases, buildings suffered serious damage and even collapsed. Most of those affected had been constructed in accordance with the Taiwanese regulations drawn up in 1982 and amplified in 1991. Few had been built in accordance with the most recent amendments (1997). In any event, while the Taiwan regulations then in force had seismic-resistant building design provisions, the fundamental problem was in their application and execution, which were not always adequate.

Taichung Tower II was still under construction on September 21, 1999. Erection of the metal framework had been completed and the curtain wall was being installed when the earthquake hit. Peak accelerations of 0.2 g were registered in the vicinity of the tower. The building, planned to withstand accelerations of up to 0.23 g with a 475 year recurrence period, survived the earthquake without appreciable damage.

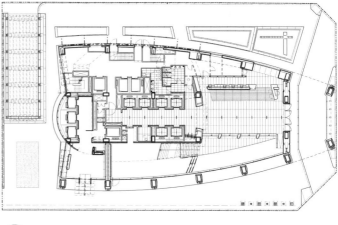

10m   0   Ground floor site plan

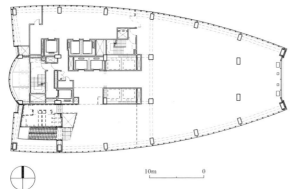

Ball room

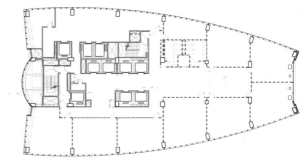

Banquet room

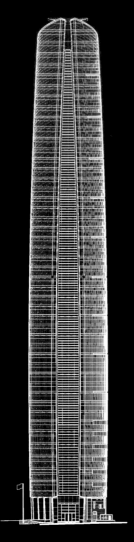

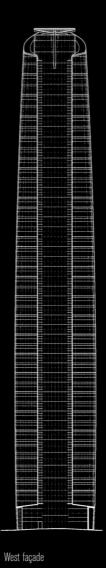

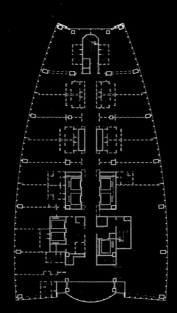

East façade

West façade

North façade

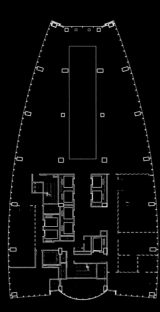

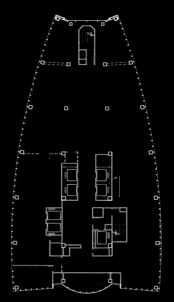

Health club floor

Guest hotel rooms floor

Restaurant floor

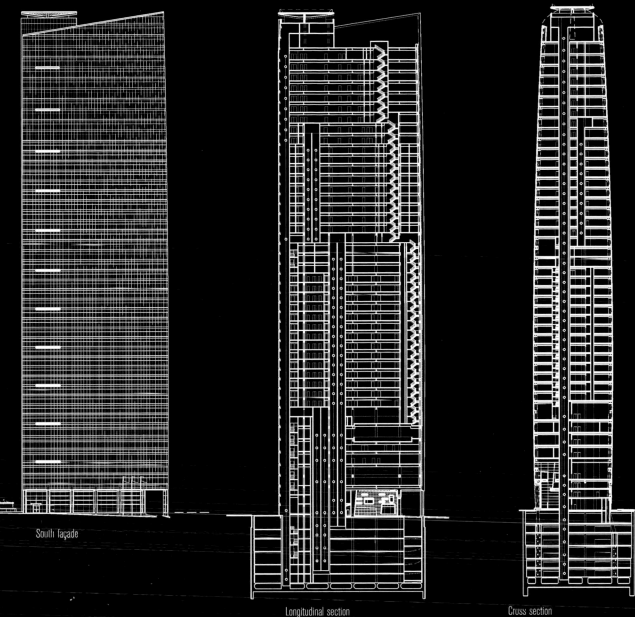

South façade

Longitudinal section

Cross section

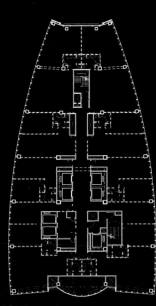

Service office floor

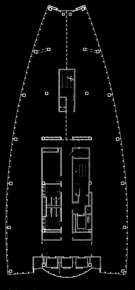

Offices floor

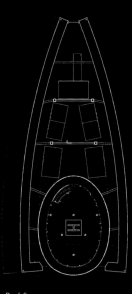

Roof floor

Bionics is a modern, interdisciplinary science that originated in the middle of the 20th Century, employing concepts from the natural and engineering sciences and synthesizing accumulated skills in such fields as biology, radio techniques, chemistry, cybernetics, physics, biophysics, and construction. It developed from the study of sophisticated load-bearing and vital systems in living beings and natural forms, analyzed from a biotechnological point of view. The bionic spirit can be summarized in the maxim: "Nature has already done it–and better."

Linnetsky, in his book, *Bionics* (1972), wrote:

Hydraulic transmission? We have it in sand. The jackhammer? We might find it in wasps. Ultrasonic radar? Bats have it. The jet engine? It functions in squids. The precision barometer? Frogs and leeches utilize it. Medusas can predict upcoming storms. The Geiger counter? Look for it in snails. Bees use a polarized solar compass. A desalinization plant? In the beak of an albatross... Living nature finds in itself all the outstanding qualities of clairvoyant builders, engineers and architects.

Javier Pioz, María Rosa Cervera & Eloy Celaya

BIONIC TOWER

Living in a vertical city

Location **Shanghai, China. Negotiations to construct the first bionic tower began with the Chinese government in early 2000** Planned construction period **15 years** Project **Cervera & Pioz, wpa** Texts and images **Cervera & Pioz, wpa**

Innovative structural material **Micro-structured High Strength Concrete (HSC),1000-2000 kg/sq. cm**
Foundation **Multiradial floating system (allows uniform force distribution and isolates the tower from direct contact with the ground)**
Seismic design **The force multifragmentation system allows absorption of seismic energy by fragmentation and controlled deformation. The dynamic-plastic isolation system acts as a barrier between the tower and ground, distributing part of the seismic energy**

Total height **4,032 feet above and 650 feet below ground**
Record **At the dawn of the 21st Century, the highest buildings are the Petronas (Kuala Lumpur), 1,478 feet. The Bionic Vertical Space (BVS) project is three times the height of the New York's Empire State Building and four times that of Paris' Eiffel Tower**
Bionic architecture **Biology + Engineering + Architecture**
Urban model **BVS city, a model for superpopulation urban growth**
Number of floors **300**
Number of inhabitants **100,000**
Total surface area **77 sq. m.**
Shape of the tower's floor plan **Elliptical and variable**
Tower's maximum floor size **545 x 410 ft.**
Base **One kilometer diameter artificial island**
Tower uses **Apartments, offices, hotels, commercial, recreational and sports complexes**
Base uses **Residential, infrastructure,**
Recurrence period considered **1,000 years**
Surface area occupied by technological systems **15-20% (depending on areas)**
Elevators **368 multiple-cabin horizontal and vertical people movers**
Horizontal and vertical speed **16-32-49 ft./second**
Scientific research **Applied bionics, begun in 1992**
Time to develop the BVS construction project **5 years**
Estimated construction time **15 years**
Total cost **approximately 11.53 billion dollars**

THE BIONIC REFERENCE POINT: TECHNOLOGY AND NATURE

THE LIMITS OF HEIGHT

architects, urban planners, and engineers have many misgivings in the face of the problems involving urban superpopulation growth and the construction of buildings of great height. Are the current urban models the right ones for the future development of megacities? At what point does the construction height of the traditional skyscraper become inappropriate? What role do we play, as inhabitants of these structures, in the design of this vertical architecture? Is it possible to create a vertical structure that does away with the belief that all skyscrapers are not humane?

These lines of thought, the result of innovative bionic scientific research, spawned the Bionic Tower. It all began in 1992 with architects Javier Pioz, Maria Rosa Cervera, and Eloy Celaya, who headed a team of scientists, designers, architects, and engineers with the firm of Cervera & Pioz. Numerous applications were developed through bionics in the field of industrial engineering, but the Bionic Tower pioneers the application of this science to human architecture.

The aim of this project is not, despite its spectacular numbers, to create the highest building ever built, but rather to find parallels between the logic of vital organic growth and the architectural, structural, and technological logic applicable to superskyscraper and megacity design. Reflecting on nature's growth processes opens up a debate on new design criteria which could be adopted in creating vertical spaces, through a fundamentally different way of seeing, understanding, and interpreting nature and the problem of building tall structures.

Analysis of the different growth systems of natural species and structures, from a blade of grass to giant trees, has made possible the discovery and development of innovations in the areas of load-bearing structures, natural air-conditioning, elevators and escalators, fluid conduits, earthquake and wind protection systems, and fire prevention and control. All of these have served to conceptually define the BVS prototype, the technological model of the Bionic Tower project.

This project's various technological innovations are important in current applications. But the line of thought involved is more important, permitting us to approach each new problem with the free spirit summed up in this bionic thought:

The architect who is trying to create a masterpiece must study nature just as the aircraft engineer studies flying beings... side by side with changing forms of nature and life there is something eternal that are the laws of beauty and harmony, which prove to be the same in nature and human life.

One of our earthly aspirations is to constantly surpass the limits of height. But, since the construction of the Empire State Building, 1,250 ft., in 1931, the highest building constructed, the Petronas Towers, in Kuala Lumpur, measures only 1480 ft. In other words, 233 ft. in 69 years. This makes the margin of vertical growth of today's skyscrapers sufficiently clear.

Most conventional skyscrapers use rigid cores and bracing screens to meet resistance problems. As a rule, the resistant material is located in large interior building cores. However, at greater building heights there is more need for load-bearing material. There is also a corresponding need for more conduits and elevators and, as the increased volume of these is proportionally greater than the linear increase in skyscraper height, it is easy to show that this model is not suitable for breaking altitude records. Thus, with conventional models above 1,300 ft., the surface and volume of structural, technological, and elevator systems, are so great that the available floor surface/space is in many cases reduced to less than 30%. For taller buildings, this free space is so greatly reduced that, without innovative approaches, the construction of a skyscraper higher than 1,640 ft. is not viable, at least in economic terms.

Let us now observe a blade of grass only a couple of inches long and a tree dozens of yards high, two organic systems responding to similar physical and chemical needs. Both depend on air, light, water, and the surrounding environment. They have the same need to rise up from the ground, supporting their own weight, resisting wind forces, internally channeling liquids up and down, and carrying out sophisticated physical and chemical processes. But the blade of grass and the tree solve these problems using very different materials, geometries, structures, and biotechnological systems.

Applying this logic to architecture, we can say that a 1 mile-high tower cannot be designed as if it were simply ten times the height of a 330 ft. tower. Nor can a megacity of 20 million inhabitants have the same urban development model as one with 2,000,000 inhabitants.

PRELIMINARY CONCLUSIONS

The first analyses and computations for the Bionic Tower prototype generated the following conclusions:

a) Horizontal loads from the wind, climatic conditions, and seismic effects are much greater than vertical loads, due to the building's own weight. Conventional structures, foundations, and seismic-resistant solutions cannot absorb these forces.

b) The interior of the complex is so large that air-conditioning by artificial means without the aid of natural factors is impractical.

c) The large number and simultaneity of escalators and elevators would overwhelm any conventional system, especially in fires and general evacuations.

Thus, the following must be considered:

1) Using material with greater resistance capacity that can provide uniformity and flexibility.

2) Developing a concept of resistant material distribution involving contribution to the shared strength of all the elements. This is necessary in order for the structure to be better balanced from the standpoints of strength, fluid conduction, and elevators and/or escalators.

3) Minimizing the dimensions of resistance components.

4) Optimizing the amount of material and the volume needed for the structure itself and its systems.

5) Optimizing the outer shell's role in resistance, due to its potential inertia.

6) Developing natural air-conditioning systems.

7) Dividing usable space and avoiding concentration of horizontal and vertical routes.

Virtual reality view of the Bionic Tower in Hong Kong Bay

THE BIONIC TOWER VERTICAL CITY, THE BVS TECHNOLOGICAL MODEL

The Bionic Tower vertical city is an immense building complex with gardens and bodies of water connected to different parts of the city through large land and rail networks, on an artificial island 1 mile wide and 660 ft. deep.

The sophisticated interior of the Bionic Tower acts as a foundation and a flexible seismic-resistant mechanism. It also contributes to the tower's multiple recycling and self-service tasks.

It is not simply an extraordinarily tall (4,032 ft.) vertical city prototype, but a dwelling of 77 square miles with 100,000 residents. Accordingly, the Bionic Tower entails an innovative urban alternative for the growth of megacities, which often suffer from a lack of usable space.

The building is organized in two main areas: the internal city and the external city. The former is designated mainly for commercial establishments, infrastructure, and cultural, recreational, and sports facilities. The latter is intended for housing, offices, hotels, and other activities requiring more natural light.

Both surround vertical gardens, the complex's natural lungs, without which it would be impossible to artificially circulate all the air needed. In this regard, the sophisticated fractal arrangement system, on which the external city is designed, allows natural air to reach the interior gardens and permits multifragmentation of wind forces.

Three hundred floors are organized into twelve 260 ft.-tall vertical neighborhoods. These are separated by hollow neutral floors which contain a large cistern, located between two areas encompassing the building systems. The cistern is supplied in a large part by rain water and humidity from the windows and contributes to the amount of potable water in the complex .

The neighborhood concept has obvious additional advantages: it permits a delineation of construction and living areas as they are completed, improving the operation's economic conditions. In addition, the neutral intermediate floors isolate the different neighborhoods from one another, facilitating escape in case of fire or general evacuation.

All the tower's areas, systems, and mechanisms are bionically supported by an innovative technological model called BVS, which can be defined as a dynamic system in equilibrium. BVS is a spatial set of polyvalent technological layers in which each component–in addition to having specific, specialized missions within the system–acts as a resistant, isolating system leading definitively to what we might call a total technological system

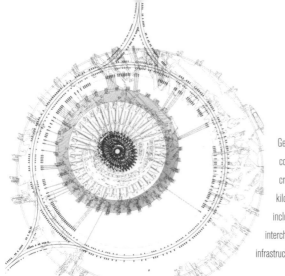

General plan of the Bionic Tower complex. The artificial island created around the tower is one kilometer in diameter and includes a transportation interchange station, residences, and infrastructural components

Layout of the two vertical cities comprising the Bionic Tower. The inner, used mainly for commercial, recreational, and cultural purposes; and the outer, with dwellings and offices

REMARKABLE CONCRETE (HSC)

In recent years, thanks to the development and use of chemical additives, high strength concrete (HSC) has come into wide use. Known as the fourth element, with the help of advanced superfluidifying agents derived from vinyl copolymers combined with plasticizers and cooled with liquid nitrogen, it has become a highly homogeneous material, several times stronger than conventional concrete.

While traditional concrete has a strength of between 200 and 400 kg/sq cm, the HSCs reach as much as 800 to 1,000 kg/sq cm. Since strength of 2,000 kg/sq cm has been achieved in the laboratory, there is no doubt that HSC will be the material of the future for building tall structures. Moreover, its great stability on impact in marine environments and in temperatures below -20 Celsius guarantee structural durability for at least 100 years.

This new material and scientific bionic developments form the theoretical basis for the BVS Bionic Tower technological model.

THE IMPORTANCE OF THE DYNAMIC VACUUM. NATURAL DILATIVE GROWTH IN PLANT STRUCTURES

In vertical plant structures, the taller the organism, the greater its inner vacuum ratio. The internal and external structural reorganization of the vacuum allows plant species to grow. While a cross-section of a young tree 4 mm in diameter is 29% vacuum, at 8 mm diameter the ratio is as much as 46%.

In the plant world this effect is achieved by structuring and hollowing its veins. Observing one of these veins under a microscope, we find that the interior of these conduits is made up of a structure of thousands of fine, connected membranes. Some of the alveoli inside these veins enclose other tiny conduits that route liquid vertically. So, a plant vein is, aside from a structure to conduct liquids, an efficacious column to support the pressure of its weight and an extraordinary column capable of absorbing traction and torsion due to the wind's dynamic action and compressions due to temperature changes. This density-reducing effect has an added benefit: it reduces excess weight from increased volume.

In plants, the role the vacuum plays in growth and structural stability is so important that it requires redefinition of the concept of the vacuum. When discussing these structures, it is more appropriate to speak of dynamic vacuum.

A tree's fluid conductor. Section of a large tree's conduit system showing the microfragmented structure that provides rigidity to the small veins conducting fluids. The average percentage of micro-vacuuming in large tree structures is on the order of 70%. This allows the conventional skyscraper concept to evolve into that of the vertical city, making it possible to surpass the 500-meter height barrier in designing the Bionic Tower.

As generally applied, the architectural concept of interior space in a conventional skyscraper has little relevance, given the repetitive character of its design techniques applied to the surface areas of each level. Contrary to the conventional skyscraper concept, which reduces interior vacuum and its potential uses, the Bionic Tower is based conceptually on a high amount of internal vacuum. This can be structured, transformed, and reorganized as different heights are reached.

DYNAMIC SYSTEMS IN EQUILIBRIUM

The human, physical, and psychological aspects of the inhabitants of a large skyscraper or a large city are extremely important. However, after a certain number of individuals, the technological aspects, such as horizontal and vertical movement, fluid channeling, resistance, air-conditioning, or air-regeneration, require innovations that force us to the conclusion that a Bionic Tower building model could be defined (in scientific terms) as a dynamic system of dynamic systems in equilibrium.

Using conventional architectural thought, we might design the vertical city by subordinating all decisions to the comfort and personal enjoyment of each individual. But employing bionic logic, it is more correct to approach the different dynamic facets of human behavior in the Bionic Tower as organized in balance with the rest of its systems. This means that each person and each household entity, the whole of the inhabitants and the complex, and the remaining dynamic systems of the building technology itself (resistance, climate, movement, etc.) can be understood as constituting a global dynamic system in equilibrium.

THE BIONIC CONCEPT OF STRUCTURE: "TOP-STRENGTH"

In most vegetable species, radial, central, and arborescent growth is present, both horizontally and vertically. This is highly suggestive of the way structure and shape interrelate, being both independent and mutually dependent. Although we can visually identify them as separate, it would be difficult to detect the line where structure becomes skin and vice-versa. This structural and formal polyvalence of living organisms is one of the strongest bionic reasons for focusing on design of the BVS as a question of a structural whole.

Computer graphics showing a dandelion with its seeds affixed to the plant's nucleus. A perfect example of "top-strength" behavior by multifragmentation of forces. The apparently chaotic structure which interconnects the filaments provides astounding strength in spite of the fragility of its components. The study of this natural structure made it possible to develop the floating cement mechanism, fundamental to the design of the foundation of the complex and its earthquake protection

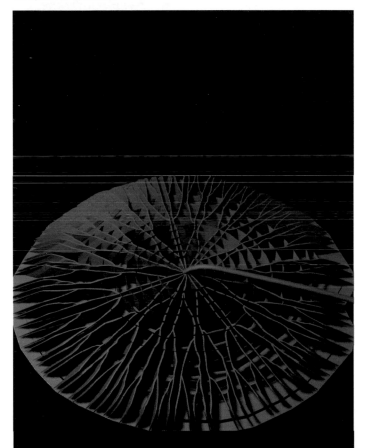

The structure of the large water lily, *Victoria regia*. In nature, a species' shape is based on its structure and on different biotechnological systems. By analogy, the shape of the Bionic Tower results from the technological development of its different dynamic systems in equilibrium with homo sapiens: a dynamic system of dynamic systems in equilibrium.

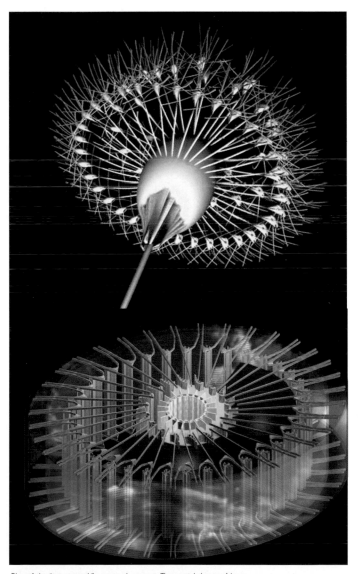

Plan of the "top-strength" structural concept. The spatial theory of layer

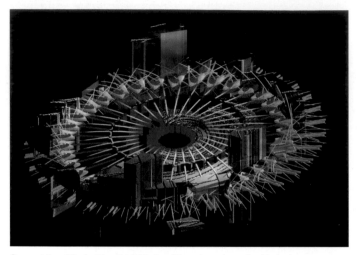

Representation of the fractal spatial distribution of the various urban and architectural areas comprising each of the twelve vertical neighborhoods. Plan of three of the 92 column-heads that link the technological systems (elevator, air-conditioning, and electrical systems) and act as vertical streets in the Bionic Tower. Dwellings will be erected on the structures forming the twelve vertical neighborhoods

Conceptually, all the pieces of the BVS architectural jigsaw puzzle work together to define the shape and the surface boundaries of the different containers, along with the load-bearing structure and technological network.

Bionic research has provided, in this regard, three novel concepts, the combination of which–in what we call the "top-strength"–configures the structural mechanism. These are the encapsulation system, the structural theory of layers, and the breathing outer shell.

ENCAPSULATION SYSTEM OR CONTAINER OF CONTAINERS

Plants can be defined as containers that house (or encapsulate) others of their kind, a definition which is verifiable independent of the scale of our analysis. The same structural use of capsules is evident in a tree trunk, a flower, a seed, or a small section of vein. This is what we call an encapsulating or continuous container system. This system affords plant species great energy savings. It reduces evaporation of liquids, rations the volume occupied, and makes possible the coexistence of many species in a small space, while providing them with additional strength, since all the circulatory or load-bearing elements, being encapsulated, contribute to force fragmentation and thus to the ability to resist wind or other forces more efficiently with very small material expenditures.

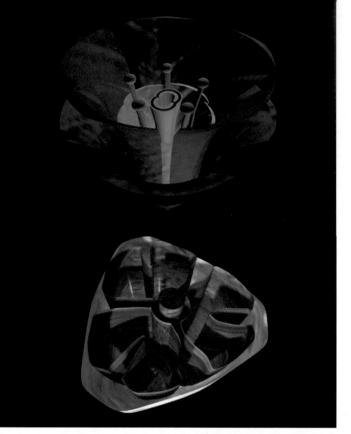

Encapsulated distribution system. Different parts of the flower encapsulate themselves inside others, reducing the useful volume without reducing its surface

Plan of a column-street, in which the natural encapsulation system is applied. Elevator capsules, fluid-conduit capsules, and electric-cabling capsules are arrayed inside the column, resulting in important volumetric savings and contributing significantly to the strength of each component

Extrapolating the container-in-a-container idea to the field of architecture, BVS can be conceived of as a continuous succession on a different scale. Applying this concept to the building as a whole, and to each of its parts, another of the keys for surpassing the structural barrier of 1,640 ft. high buildings was discovered.

The conventional skyscraper model considers all structural systems (columns, beams, metalwork), conduits (air-conditioning, water, electricity), and elevator shafts as independent, even spatially separated systems. In the Bionic Tower, however, each of the capsules comprising the main structure uses a continuous container system to house the different load-bearing fluid and transport mechanisms. In this way, the electrical, air-conditioning, and water networks are placed inside the hermetic capsules situated inside the communications system capsules of the strengthened columns.

The encapsulated (or use-shared) volume system makes it possible to optimize non-pedestrian surfaces, providing great cost savings. This also acts as a "top-strength" trabeation system. Moreover, looking at the vertical structure as a container housing conduits which are also structured allows us to see them not as thick, solid components but as hollow pieces made up of fine membranes that increase the size of the section carrying the load without increasing the weight. With the same amount of material, capsule fragmentation and layout make possible trabeate behavior ten times as effective as the conventional approach of connecting material in large, solid elements. They also provide the complex with extraordinary flexibility, a major benefit in terms of stability in the face of seismic and wind activity.

This capsule system also significantly conserves the volume and surface area used for building systems. The Bionic Tower technological systems need only 15-20% of the building area, compared with 50-60% in conventional skyscrapers.

Besides, the Tower's maximum spire oscillation is only 4 ft. in each direction (the same as the Empire State Building), with a minimum oscillation frequency. And this system's polyvalence allows for evolution of the different technological processes during the 15-year period needed for container construction

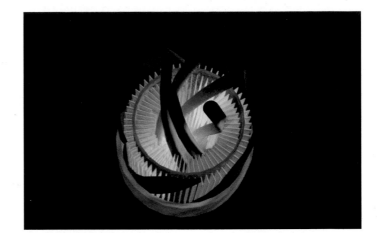

Diagram of the helicoidal arrangement of a tree structure, which permits efficient absorption of torsional effects

The 92 capsules are organized into three concentric column-heads running the full height of the tower. The containers of the different structures are progressively built onto the column-defining capsules. As the different vertical neighborhoods are erected, construction is rotated in a double helicoid direction. Thus, the tensions produced by expanding the different layers of the structure are able to compensate for each other. The hollow neutral areas between the vertical neighborhoods are comprised of a multi-radial structure that ties the 92 capsule-columns together and permits the trabeate complex itself to behave like a unitary flexible mechanism.

STRUCTURAL LAYER THEORY

To the naked eye, a severed tree appears as if it has grown in diameter by adding concentric rings. But there are important mechanisms applicable to vertical growth, such as the double helicoid fiber arrangement, which are key factors in the tree's resistance to the extraordinary amounts of wind torsion and flexion. The fibers of trees are organized in two crossed helicoidal fibrous structures, so the tree, tending to rotate in a certain direction, uses part of its structure like beams, easily absorbing the forces of tension. When the tree tends to rotate in the opposite direction, the rest of the structure is subjected to the tension. In this way, the tree is able to absorb great tensional and torsional forces using a small amount of material, obviating the need to excessively increase its mass.

These plants grow in layers that alternate between elements in a radial arrangement and elements in a lineal configuration. In other words, they combine specialized layers for structural fibrous behavior and others for fluid conduits. The latter, in addition to following the aforementioned helicoidal growth principle, possess a fractal geometric order, the principle of growth common to all plant species, with very important advantages from the standpoint of transformation, load-carrying, and isolation.

If we add up the amount of microvacuum inside each vein, along with the microvacuums located between the interconnections of different layers, we find that 75% of the structure of a tree is empty space. A vacuum, in other words, which in spite of the small diameter involved is the real actor in bearing the stress.

THE BREATHING SHELL

As the tree grows, the inner veins transporting its vital fluids atrophy and begin shaping the woody core. At the same time, the more perimetral vertical conduits multiply while diminishing in size. The smaller and more numerous they are, the farther from the center will they be. Thus, we can say that the conduits (vascular bundles) make up a second skin parallel to the bark (or plant cortex). This second skin is a strong support because of the large amount of microstructure (an authentic defense mechanism against fires in large plant structure.

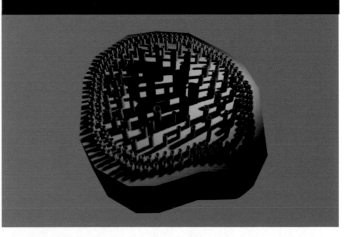

Representation of the perimetric organization of an arboreal structure's veins, the multiplication of which provides great additional stress-bearing capacity

This thought led to another of the principal innovations in developing the BVS concept. As a general rule, a skyscraper's facade is conceived as a passive membrane separating interior and exterior. This also allows for certain thermal, light, and acoustic insulation. Air-conditioning systems generally operate on this membrane to heat and cool it so it serves as a climatic filter.

BVS defines the facade as an active, micro-structured element permitting organization of the complex's perimetric city, including the use of load-bearing technological and climatic systems. Thus, the whole tower complex is encapsulated in a final perimetric container defined by a fractal (nest type) micro-structured aluminum element. This outer shell is highly versatile because of its resistance and flexibility and because of its capacity to multi-fragment external wind forces and seismic vibrations.

The BVS shell breathes, simulating a natural chaotic fractal mechanism such as those frequently found in trees and birds. As in plants, the first large BVS container would be the building's facade. Certainly, the approach employing this primary container enveloping the vertical space and its architectural, structural, and technological relationship to the other containers is one of the most important innovations of the BVS design.

Air circulates throughout the BVS complex perimeter in a carefully regulated way. This helps reduce the building's wind resistance and maintain a stable microclimate of natural air inside the complex. Thus, the components needed to heat and cool the internal spaces are reduced while internal gardens ("green lungs") blossom with the hypertrophic growth vegetation undergoes due to the greenhouse effect.

THE FLOATING CEMENT MECHANISM AND FLEXIBLE ANTI-SEISMIC ISOLATION

Bionically speaking, trees are not supported in the ground, they float, suspended in the chaotic structure made up of their thousands of roots. These are called nest structures and, because of their capacity to multi-fragment forces, both in terms of magnitude and direction, they enjoy enormous strength and flexibility. To devise the appropriate anti-seismic system for the Bionic Tower, the anchoring systems of large trees were analyzed. These biotechnological systems combine various complementary mechanisms.

For one thing, the encapsulation mechanism with which the root organizes its different technological systems converts these elements into powerful columns capable of absorbing great tensions. For another, the area occupied by the roots extends for dozens of meters from the trunk—like an inverted umbrella—thus distributing the stress. Where they meet the trunk, the roots are transformed into strong basal ribs which, as in the case of the fuma tree (165 feet tall), can extend up to 16 feet. Besides, the roots of these large trees hypertrophy its bark and fragment its perimeter with deep cuts so that, while considerably increasing surface contact with the ground, they also increase its strength through friction.

The combination of liquid and microstructured plates makes possible perfect load-bearing behavior using a small amount of material. The system of multi-fragmentation of forces present in most natural species was used to create the foundation and seismic-resistant systems of the Bionic Tower

The multiradial floating system foundation

The behavior of the foundation and seismic-resistant systems was one of the most significant concerns of the Bionic Tower project, and the ingenious solution has proved to be highly satisfactory.

The bionic concept of anchoring a structure to the ground, as used by large trees such as the fuma or the obeche, aided the development of the multiradial floating system. By conceptual analogy, the Bionic Tower is united with the ground, floating inside different multiradial structures that multi-fragment stresses. This is one of the principal reasons for the existence of the additional perimetric area surrounding the tower.

The suspended subsystem described above has a significant additional advantage: as the tower is separated from direct contact with the ground by numerous hollow filaments that serve as interconnecting passageways among different areas in the base, the floating foundation mechanism behaves like an effective plastic isolator between building and terrain, helping (by multifragmenting stresses) to damp seismic effects.

The artificial perimetric lakes, which make the base area seem like a large maritime transport hub, complete the earthquake-resistant mechanism. They are comprised of water and thin membranes with a fractal organization similar to the internal structure of a citrus fruit.

This mixed bionic structure displays a high capacity to absorb vibrations and transform energies. Besides, the tower's willowy profile (1/10-1/20), made possible by its revolutionary structural system, permits great plasticity (controlled deformation), ideal for damping measures.

There is a natural principle involving maximum material and energy savings. Natural shapes are not generated by precise, predetermined geometries, but by flexible laws of growth that allow modification of species' structures and shapes which adapt them to climatic conditions, in both their immediate surroundings and their microhabitat. This concept is present in the design of the Bionic Tower: its earthquake-resistant mechanism, which involves the principle of force microfragmentation, can be adapted to the seismic requirements of each area.

The solution to the foundation problem: a multiradial floating system

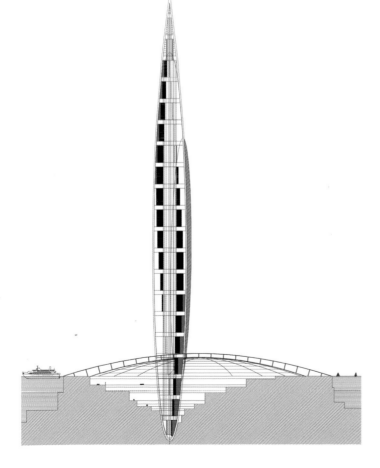

Section showing the helicoidal distribution of the vertical neighborhoods and the tower's ground anchorage. The tower's own weight and the wind's lateral forces on the surfaces are so great that it was essential to develop a new subsystem concept. The result is inspired by the grasping technique of the root systems of large trees. The innovative multiradial floating system works like giant bicycle wheels, arranged stepwise to create a 650 ft. deep inverted cone with a maximum diameter of one kilometer. The tower is anchored on its axis. This structure also serves other equally important functions: a seismic-resistant system (absorbing vibrations) with the tower not in direct contact with the ground, an urban container where the tower-city's most important services will be located, and an for all the dynamic communications systems

Glossary

ACCELERATION. Variation in velocity per unit of time, expressed as the former derived from velocity or the latter derived from displacement with respect to time. Ground acceleration is more important than ground displacement during an earthquake because the latter is more directly related to the effect of force. From a civil engineering standpoint, it is of interest to know, through accelerograms, the peak accelerations, because this parameter combined with mass yields forces, forces yield deformations, deformations yield stresses, and stresses, if very high, can cause a building to collapse.

ACCELEROGRAM. Record, against time, of ground accelerations caused by an earthquake, obtained through the use of accelerographs.

ACCELEROGRAPH. Instrument used to record and graphically study the acceleration of a movement, such as that caused by an earthquake. An accelerograph registers in areas of high frequency, where acceleration occurs.

AFTERSHOCK. Smaller earthquake that follows a larger (main) one.

AMPLITUDE. (See *VIBRATION*.)

BASE. The floor of a building structure, which seismic movement is considered to reach.

DAMPING. The capacity to dissipate ground-generated energy. As deformation increases, so does damping. (See VIBRATION)

EARTHQUAKE. Shaking or abrupt movement of the terrestrial crust, produced by the sudden liberation of mechanical energy accumulated in the areas close to the surface of the Earth. Earthquakes move in seismic waves, causing a series of vibrations in the ground. Ninety percent of earthquakes originate in cracks in the crust's solid rock in seismic zones. These cracks (faults) occur when pressures inside the Earth increase—sometimes over millions of years—to the point where the crust can no longer sustain them. The crust and surface then abruptly seek a new equilibrium position: an earthquake occurs. The causes of such seismic events in general, then, are tectonic, either because of displacement of one rocky surface over another, or the collision of two plates. The tectonic plates, about 100 kilometers thick, move 2 to 20 cm a year. Other types of earthquakes (some 10%) originate because of the shifting of underground spaces due to material above them or because of human activities such as explosions. The remaining 7% are volcanic.

EPICENTER. The point on the Earth's surface located above the hypocenter or focus of an earthquake. Because it is at times very difficult to locate this point with precision, an epicentral zone is sometimes considered.

FAULT. A fracture or break in the Earth's crust and surface where blocks of rock have been displaced. Faults are produced by tectonic forces of compression, decompression, or tangency and are accompanied by vertical, horizontal, or oblique displacements. Earthquakes have a certain likelihood of recurring in pre-existing faults.

FLEXIBILITY. (See *RIGIDITY*.)

FOCUS. (See *HYPOCENTER*.)

FORESHOCK. Small earthquake which in some cases is present prior to the main seismic episode.

FREQUENCY. (See *VIBRATION*.)

HYPOCENTER OR FOCUS. The subsurface location where an earthquake is believed to have originated. Earthquakes are grouped into three types according to focal depth: superficial (less than 6 miles below the surface), intermediate (between 65 and 275 miles), and deep (more than 275 miles).

INTENSITY. Subjective description of the apparent effects caused by an earthquake. It is used to evaluate specific manifestations of seismic ground shaking (people's reactions, degree of destruction to buildings, and soil disturbances such as breaks, fractures, slides, cave-ins, etc.) to describe an earthquake's destructive potential at a certain site. Various intensities may be established for the same earthquake, since the determination depends on the evaluation site and the assessment of the person studying the effects. Intensity is highest at the epicenter and decreases with distance. It depends, first, on the earthquake's magnitude, that is, on its intrinsic violence, and, second, on the depth at which the epicenter is located. Thus, for the same magnitude, the closer an earthquake is to the surface, the more intense it is.

LIQUEFACTION. Phenomenon by which solid ground temporarily loses its ability to support loads and behaves like a dense fluid with little resistance to lateral movements, normally caused by vibrations such as those that occur during an earthquake.

MAGNITUDE. Parameter measuring the size of an earthquake in terms of the energy released in the form of seismic waves during the rupture of a fault. It is independent of the observation site. Significantly, an earthquake has only one measure of magnitude and different measures of intensity. Magnitude may be considered a tremor's relative size and is determined by taking the logarithm (base 10) of the maximum amplitude of some kind of wave movement (P, superficial) and applying to it a correction factor of epicentral distance and focal depth. The most common measures of magnitude are those of the Richter (or local) scale, M, of body waves (Mb), of surface waves (Ms) and moment magnitude (Mw). The first three are determined by measuring the greatest amplitude of the waves on a seismograph. The other is related to the physical characteristics of torque.

MODIFIED MERCALLI SCALE. Non-mathematically based scale of intensity which assigns different levels from I to XII (imperceptible, very light, light, moderate, rather strong, strong, very strong, destructive, highly destructive, disastrous, catastrophic, totally catastrophic) to building damage, generation of natural phenomena, and the way a tremor is felt by people. For example, intensity I is described as "not felt except by a very few under especially favorable conditions." Similarly, intensity XII corresponds to almost total damage, in other words, "landslides and rockfalls, objects thrown into the air, lines of sight and level distorted."

MSK SCALE. Scale created by Medredev, Sponheuer, and Karnik in 1964 to measure earthquake intensity. Divided into twelve magnitudes (not felt, scarcely felt [very light], partially or uncertainly felt, clearly felt, awakening, fright, damage to buildings, destruction of buildings, generalized damage to buildings, generalized destruction of buildings, destruction, changes in terrain levels), it determines more precisely than the Modified Mercalli the effects an earthquake has on buildings. Damage begins to be notable after intensity VII. This scale is used in Europe.

PERIOD. (See *VIBRATION.*)

PLATE. Each of the relatively stable, continually moving, large segments of rigid rock that make up the terrestrial crust and upper mantle. There are six enormous plates: the Euro-Asiatic, African, American, Antarctic, Indo-Australian, and Pacific). There are other, smaller plates, such as the Cocos plate in the Caribbean.

RECURRENCE INTERVAL. Approximate period between earthquakes in a given seismic zone.

RESONANCE. (See *VIBRATION.*)

RICHTER SCALE OR LOCAL MAGNITUDE. Mathematically based scale that measures earthquake magnitude. Developed by Charles Richter in 1935, it is also known today by the name local magnitude. Although it is the most commonly known and used scale of magnitude, it is not always the most appropriate one for describing earthquake size. Richter defined the magnitude of a local seismic event as the "base 10 logarithm of the maximum amplitude of the seismic wave (in thousandths of a millimeter) recorded on a standard seismograph located at a distance of 60 miles from the seismic epicenter." This means that each time the magnitude increases one unit, the amplitude of the seismic wave increases 10 times. And, since logarithmic magnitudes are involved, to raise the magnitude of an earthquake by one it would be necessary to multiply the released energy by 33, and to raise it by two, it would be necessary to release 1,000 times more energy. Although the largest earthquake recorded to date reached a magnitude of 9.5, a fissure some 900 miles long and 150 miles wide causing an average displacement of 65 ft., the Richter scale is open at both ends. In fact, at the opposite extreme of the scale, negative magnitudes have been achieved in the laboratory with millimetric fissures.

The Richter Scale

Magnitude	Average number of earthquakes in a year
8 and above	1
7 to 7.9	18
6 to 6.9	120
5 to 5.9	800
4 to 4.9	6,200 (estimated)
3 to 3.9	49,000 (estimated)
2 to 3	1,000 per day
1 to 2	8,000 per day

Although magnitude and intensity scales measure different aspects of an earthquake and are independent, for superficial earthquakes (those occurring at a depth of 40 to 50 miles) there is an empirical relationship between magnitude and intensity.

Magnitude (Richter scale)	Intensity (Modified Mercalli scale)	Amount of TNT
2	I-II	650 kg
3	III-IV	20 tons
4	V	625 tons
5	VI- VII	20,000 tons
6	VII-VIII	625,000 tons
7	IX-X	20,000,000 tons
8	XI-XII	625 megatons

RIGIDITY. Resistance to deformation. Non-rigid structures are called flexible.

RISK. The degree of likelihood of loss due to some potential danger.

SEISMIC EVENT. (See *EARTHQUAKE.*)

SEISMIC ZONES. The world's main seismic zones coincide with the boundaries of the tectonic plates and with the position of the Earth's active volcanoes. This reflects the fact that the cause of earthquakes and volcanic eruptions is closely related to the planet's tectonic process.

SEISMICITY. Degree of frequency and intensity of earthquakes affecting a given region of the Earth. The highest seismicity, expressed in terms of the number of ground-shaking events in a region over the course of a year per 9,300,000 sq. ft. of surface area, is in Japan, Chile, Peru, and New Zealand.

SEISMOGRAM. The record of earthquakes obtained by a seismograph. The instrument registers waves in zones of intermediate frequency, where velocity dominates. Knowing the seismograms of different stations makes it possible to determine the epicenter and focus of an earthquake.

SEISMOGRAPH. Instrument for measuring the amplitude, duration, time, and other important parameters of movements at a certain point on the Earth's crust.

TECTONIC PLATES (THEORY OF). In 1912, Alfred Wegener suggested that the twelve large zones of the Earth's crust and upper mantle, called tectonic plates, are in continual motion and that all the continents come from a single original mass of rock called Pangaea which existed approximately 200 million years ago. Over time, Pangaea began to break up due to large earthquakes and the resulting enormous blocks began to drift apart, giving rise to the formation of the continents, which are still subject to movement.

TSUNAMI. A gigantic ocean wave or series of waves caused by a major disturbance on the ocean floor. Seaquakes occur when an abrupt movement deep in the ocean or on the ocean floor displaces a great mass of water. This is generally due to underwater tectonic shifting, although it is occasionally caused by the collapse of a volcanic crater at or just below sea level, or the caving in of a volcano's slopes. The literal translation of Japanese term is "large waves in ports.

VIBRATION. The cyclical, rhythmic movement of a body. It occurs when the body is displaced from its neutral position and seeks to return to the previous equilibrium point. The magnitude of lineal displacement from the neutral position is called amplitude. The time required to complete a cycle is called a period. The number of cycles per second is known as frequency. The effects that tend to reduce the amplitude of successive cycles are referred to as damping or absorption. The increase in amplitude of successive cycles is the resonance effect. If the period of a soil deposit coincides with the period of vibration of some structure built on it, the seismic waves coming out of the rock will be greatly amplified.